Run Amuck

Environmentalism
And
Government

Run Amuck

By:

Tiffany Montaño

Dedication:

For BooBoo
With love

Tiffany Montaño

Table of Contents:

The Pig Farm 1

The Ultimate Gas Tax 6

Protecting the Environment 10

The Year of the Frog................................. 13

The Mortgage Meltdown 25

Oil and Energy.. 44

Automobile Bailout 53

Free Trade and NAFTA............................. 65

Star Gazing 68

Smoke and Mirrors.................................... 77

Defense and Religion.................................. 89

Guilt by Association 103

Medicare and Healthcare........................ 117

The Media R.I.P. 123

Voter Ignorance and Gay Marriage.......... 130

Trust Me.. 148

Death of a Nation.................................... 153

Not an Option... 166

Epilog: 169

Preface:

You probably know where your children are tonight but do you know where your taxes are?

Introduction:

Like most Americans I believe in protecting the environment, our most precious asset. I spent my life as an environmentalist. At one point my life insurance beneficiary was The Mono Lake Committee, an organization that is dedicated to protecting one of the rarest lakes from extinction through water diversion to Southern California.

I was an environmentalist until the radical segment took over and forced bad economic and environmental policies on the American public in the name of the environment. I have long dropped my membership in the Mono Lake Committee and other more radical groups like The Sierra Club and The Nature Conservancy.

I once believed in these groups along with the scientists and the government to protect the environment. To do the right thing. Not only for the Spotted Owl and the California Red Legged Frog but also for mankind. I ask you when is the death of one frog more important than the life or death of one human being? There must be a balance between the needs of animals, insects, snakes, spiders and the needs of man. The animals have taken over and they are running the zoo and are ***running Amuck***.

The environmentalist movement appears to want us to go back to living like our forefathers, in wickiups, teepees and log cabins. They want us to demolish hydroelectric and water storage dams and restore the rivers and streams to their pre-dammed conditions. They have no concept of living off the utility grid, forgoing their lattes and air conditioners and even worse, they don't understand the flooding that occurred before many of these dams and levees were built. Flooding that annually demolished cities like Los Angeles, Sacramento and New Orleans. They have no understanding of what life was like before to the residences of these small towns. We have sustained energy because we built these dams, and we also maintain erosion control, a water supply for areas that were once arid, a thriving fish and recreation industry and agriculture. We are able to water the land to feed the masses.

Many of these people are well intentioned, uninformed, trusting and too busy with meeting the needs of their daily lives to expend much of their time thinking about these issues. Yes they want to protect the Polar Bear. They're cute. Who wouldn't to protect the Polar Bear or the deer herds? Other so called environmentalists use the environment as a way to line their pockets through speaking engagements and employment. Like former assistant director of the FBI Mark Felt (Deep Throat) said during the Nixon Administration, "Follow the Money."

The most dangerous environmentalist is the true believer. He truly believes the spotted owl, the snakes and frogs, the rats and rodents should be protected at all costs.

When does the need of a frog supersede the needs of a mankind? If being an environmentalist in this day and age means sacrificing one human life to save one frog, then I have become an anti-environmentalist.

Illustrations:

The Politician cover art and all 2008
California wildfire photographs by:

Tiffany Montaño

Photograph of Tiffany Montaño by:

Doreen Erhardt

Disclaimer:

The views express within are the sole
views of the writer and may or may not agree
with your views.

Run Amuck

The Pig Farm
The Care and Feeding of a Politician

The politician is the rarest of endangered species therefore must be protected and cared for properly at all costs. Before adopting a politician it is important to understand the breed. Often inexperienced voters buy into a politician's rhetoric with little understanding of the breed's policies. Rather selecting their politician because of only one policy. Most voters have little understanding of their selections true beliefs and standings. There are two basic pure breeds of politicians and numerous hybrids, mixes or mongrel breeds. The basic two breeds are the Democrats, a socialistic breed that supports wealth distribution in the form of higher taxes on the top 5% of taxpayers and a welfare payment to the bottom 40%. The Democrat supports more government as only government can fix the problems of the masses and higher taxes while distracting the taxpayer with empty promises of personal rights and free healthcare. The Democrat rarely understands basic economics and often proposes billions of dollars in pork barrel spending. The Democrat is most often the radical environmentalist who preaches environmentalism while lining their pocket with hard earned tax dollars and speaking engagement fees. The Democrat chastises the Detroit executives for private jet use while flying in their own taxpayer sponsored jets.

The purebred Republican supports less government. The Republican Breed also supports lower taxes and owner retained wealth. This policy is better known as Trickledown Economics. A term which during the 2008 election took on negative connotations became a Democrat's negative catch term. This term was associated with the outgoing administration and therefore was tied to a Republican President who was strong armed by a Democratic Congress for the last two years of his administration. The basic explanation of Trickledown Economics is that the wealthy create the jobs and if you give tax breaks and incentives to the wealthy they will do the right thing and create jobs. This is frequently accomplished when a state or city gives tax credits to a business as an incentive to locate in their state or neighborhood rather than locating their plant overseas. Now frankly I would rather see Detroit get jobs than China where

Chrysler is building a new plant, while at the same time accepting billions of dollars from the taxpayer.

Until the advent of Day-traders as a result of the internet, Wall Street was primarily Republican.

As I have said these are the purebreds, but most politicians are not purebred but rather are a mix. Part Conservative, part Liberal, part Democrat part Republican.

Too often a politician is adopted because he is cute and cuddly, a Republican or Democrat and even sometimes adopted or not based upon gender and color of skin. When selecting a politician extreme care should be taken when considering experience. Experience is preferred but sometimes inexperience allows the possibility of paper training.

If not properly vetted this species has been known to turn on its owner. Its bite is not only painful; it is extremely expensive to treat and often becomes festered. It should be noted here that over 60% of all politicians turn on and bite their owner. This should be taken into consideration when considering a politician and extreme caution should be used before buying or adopting any politician. Choice of this breed may best be left to the professionals.

The mainstay of the politician's diet is pork. The average politician will throughout a lifetime consume copious amounts of pork in the form of pork barrel spending projects, auto and economic bailouts, stimulus packages and bridges to nowhere. It should be noted the *politician has a voracious appetite and cannot be overfed.* The politician can however be underfed. When underfed the politician will begin showing signs of malnutrition, rapidly becoming delusional and will soon begin consuming massive vats of Kool-Aid. Signs of malnutrition in the typical politician are denial and lies. He often says "I forgot", and appears dazed and confused. He rapidly becomes addicted to his Kool-Aid and soon overdoses. He begins chanting 95% tax reduction. Over and over like a mantra. His eyes glaze over. He becomes obsessed. He sees everything as fodder. He gathers together his fellow same breed politicians and together they find ways into the grain silo (budget) and soon consumes everything in sight. It should be noted the *politician has been known to be cannibalistic.* Eventually he finds his way back into the pig farm (Congress) where he finishes off billions of tax dollars in pork. Soon he spews forth massive amounts of methane gas from multiple orifices. Eventually he outlives his usefulness and sits unconscious at his Senate or House seat, taking the place of a younger, possibly clearer thinking Politician. The Politician can live up to 100 years with rapidly decreasing usefulness.

This is the lifespan of the typical Politicians.

It should be noted that the EPA is both owner and trainer of the politician including the top dog, the Commander and Chief, the President of the United States and has full control of what he and we can do. The EPA pulls the strings with the precision of a master puppeteer.

The Ultimate Gas Tax

A recent news report said the EPA, a group of appointed Politians, wanted to expand its powers and impose a fine on any rancher that raised a farm animal that produced large amounts of methane gas. Under this program the fine was to be $175.00 per cow. Now any clear thinking person would have to ask themselves what would this do to the price of beef, pork, cheese, chicken, turkey or milk? In many cases it would put the small rancher, pig farmer and poultry breeder out of business. Then what? In order to comply with the EPA's demands we would have a choice to either slaughter all the cows or turn them loose? If you turn them loose, they will still produce the same amount of methane gas that the EPA says is contributing to the greenhouse gasses. So the alternative would be that the ranchers would be forced to slaughter their cattle. If the EPA has its way that is.

So what would the end result be? If you slaughter the cattle to reduce green house gasses you would initially have a glut of meat on the market, meat prices would drop, more farmers would go out of business and the industry would collapse. Under this scenario people would starve. Then you would have malnutrition, death and disease while the politician just gets fatter on his speaking fees. Granted, this is worse case scenario but think about it. Eventually we would have to put cattle, pigs, chickens etc. on the endangered species list.

Who can forget the 1987 garbage barge Mobro cruising off the eastern coast from Long Island to Belize and back with the environmentalists saying we didn't have room to dispose of our garbage and by 2010 the whole nation would be knee deep in garbage. It seems we came up with a solution, we burned the garbage. One solution to the methane gas issue is to capture and use most of the methane produced. This can and is being done at some of the newer public dump sites. Other sites burn their garbage. Why don't we generate energy with the garbage we burn?

My friend's family put the idea of generating energy from methane produced chicken waste to work at his egg ranch. He filled up his swimming pool with chicken waste, covered it and used the methane produced to run his generators. When the manure was spent he pumped it out and refilled the swimming pool, having through his methane producing, green house gas emitting poultry an almost inexhaustible source of clean renewable energy.

Scientists announce methane gas is found on Mars. Methane that they say can be used as rocket fuel. Then why don't we use methane as rocket fuel? Mankind is being blamed for global warming yet the Pacific Ocean belches methane gas at 20,000 ton per belch. That is larger than the footprint that the Obama coronation and mankind's footprint combined. So we are being told to believe that we humans are the cause of global warming..

In all seriousness we do have a bigger more imminent problem than global warming if it really does exist. That problem is with the farmers and their inability to get financing to plant their crops. Crops need to be planted in early spring and if the farmers don't get much needed loans they will not be able to plant next year's food products. President-elect Obama has pledged to put an end to farm subsidies. Not the tax dollars going toward reclaiming rice fields to rebuild mounds for snake habitat but subsidies to the farmers who produce our food supply. I don't understand it, do you? It would seem to me food is more relevant than snake habitat.

Perhaps we should forget about the cow gas tax and put one on all the politicians instead. After all, with all the bull in Washington they put more methane into the air than all the automobiles, diesel trucks, smokestacks, coal burning power plants, cows, pigs, chickens and other animals in the world combined.

Protecting the Environment

Who is the EPA anyway? The following is an excerpt from their website. *"EPA leads the nation's environmental science, research, education and assessment efforts. The mission of the Environmental Protection Agency is to protect human health and the environment. Since 1970, EPA has been working for a cleaner, healthier environment for the American people."*[1]

But if you begin to look into their policies and the partnership, the EPA has aligned itself with the radical element of the environmentalist movement. If you look at the policies put in place under their watch you will see that they no longer protect human health.

2008 was not only the beginning of an economic drought but also a very real water shortage year. The culmination of over ten years of drought brought many of our lakes and dams at their lowest levels in history. California Governor Schwarzenegger proposed building three new water storage dams. These Dams would have generated electricity as well as water storage. The

---

[1] http://www.epa.gov;

environmentalists or as it was reported in the news, the Democratic Senate (of California) said no you cannot build any more dams in California, you need to "Conserve." With a growing population and no rain in sight it becomes a little difficult to conserve. Californians did conserve, they quit watering their landscape. Then when the wildfires burned throughout California, over 2000 wildfires, many homes were lost that might have been saved if they would have had a green belt around them.

We should all conserve. The Native American way of life was to only take what you need. And not to waste the resources the Great Spirit gave us. But the settlers chose to annihilate both indigenous inhabitants and animals. Killing off both the Native American and his primary of source food, the Bison. Ancient history, so let us look at today's reality. Unless, California and in reality America develops a Chinese policy of zero population growth, there is only so much conservation you can accomplish. Where do you conserve? You have quit watering your lawn. Do you quit taking showers or flushing the toilet? Then you have sanitation problems. And health problems too.

You may wonder why the Democrats don't want to build dams, especially when their President-elect wants to invest billions of tax dollars rebuilding the infrastructure. The environmentalists have said building a dam might affect the deer populations. It's the cute effect here. Don't relocate or displace Bambi, and in the mean time your children are starving because there is no food because there is no water for the farmers to raise food products.

The Year of the Frog

The environmentalists declared 2008 the year of the frog.

The California Red Legged Frog could be considered the replacement to the Spotted Owl as the poster child of the environmental movement.

Supposedly the California Red Legged Frog is the frog Mark Twain wrote about in the story about the Calaveras County Frog Jumping Contest. Or that is what we are being led to believe but the real story is just a little bit different. A recent article in the Calaveras Enterprise says the following;

"Basey came under fire from several people for his claim that the red-legged frog was the famed jumping frog from Mark Twain's "The Celebrated Jumping Frog of Calaveras County." Basey set the record straight after the meeting.

"In the 1970s, it dawned on me that if there was any truth to the Mark Twain story the winner of that contest would have to be the red-legged frog because bullfrogs did not exist in California until 1922," he said. "I was making presentations across the state at that time, and said the jumping frog was a

red-legged frog to make my speeches more interesting.""

So that is how the California Red Legged Frog came to be the *fabled* frog represented in Mark Twain's story. Everybody seems to forget Mark Twain was a fiction writer, not a frog biologist and therefore the story of the Calaveras County Frog Jumping Contest and the amount of frogs that existed could just as easily have been creative license.

My husband David used to live in the area and as a musician performed during the Calaveras County Frog Jumps at the Avery Hotel. We have a lot of history in Calaveras County. He tried to open a fried frog leg stand at the Frog Jumps and even though they would have been bull frog legs, the local citizens acted as if he wanted to kill the bald eagle. Everybody else thought it was a great idea.

In front of one hotel in a little town called Volcano, California the locals sit around and spit on their quarters to bet on who's quarter the fly will land on first. If I write the story the Flies of Volcano, would those flies, in a hundred years or so, be considered endangered? Should we then put the house fly on the endangered species list?

The people of Calaveras County are good, hard working people but most are not rocket scientists. They are up in arms over the California Red Legged Frog and the environmental issues that have prevented from trout being stocked in their local lakes.

In all difference to Mr. Basey, there may very well have been frog jumping contests in Mark Twain's day or just as likely Mark Twain, (Samuel Clemens) saw two frogs and two children playing with the frogs and came up with the idea for the *fabled* frog jumping contest. But contest or not, that still doesn't guarantee these frogs were the California Red Legged Frog, the California Yellow Legged Frog or just a mix of tree frogs and toads. Reports say these frogs were eaten by the thousands and made their way onto the menu at the finer restaurants in San Francisco. I contend they therefore couldn't be the California Red Legged Frog because the California Red Legged Frog is only 2 to 5 inches long. There is not much meat on those legs. It would be more like eating toothpicks.

California currently has 309 identified endangered or threatened species and over 33,000 listed sites. It has gotten out of control. Is everything in California to be deemed protected, threatened or endangered? Everything except mankind that is. I guess to the environmental movement humans aren't important.

One of the biggest drains on the California budget and constraint to construction is the environmental issues forced upon the taxpayers and developers by the uninformed do-gooders that have become the mainstay of the environmental movement. Environmentalists who sit in their air conditioned office, using their computers, unwilling to actually investigate sites that they want assessed. Taxpayers spend millions of dollars on California Red Legged and Yellow Legged Frog assessments and surveys, building beaver dams, snake habitats and fish ladders to help the salmon spawn. But just like the dinosaurs some species are destined to die off. How different this world would be if the dinosaurs would have survived the ice age. The environmentalists would be trying to protect them too.

Recently the California Fish and Wildlife Service has been prohibited from stocking fish in many lakes and streams in California because there was no environmental impact study done when they first started stocking these lakes and streams over 100 years ago. Of course we didn't have the EPA or the eco-nuts then. A judge in San Francisco issued a moratorium on stocking the lakes until this issue can be resolved through surveying over 1000 lakes and streams at millions of tax dollars. This will potentially collapse an entire industry. Not only the fishing industry but also tourism. People will be prevented from sport fishing and even just enjoying nature. Will Californians be prohibited from entering areas where California Red Legged Frogs are found? Areas which environmentalists have reportedly stocked with the California Red Legged Frog. If you read the CRLF site survey information it will. You are not allowed to take a species. Taking of a species is described as harassing or disturbing them in any manner. Why? The California Red Legged Frog is not even endangered but is listed as possibly threatened. It lives 10 years and produces 2000 to 6000 eggs. They have recently been found in areas they were thought to be extinct, but more likely they have simply migrated. Or were planted. In response to a recent site assessment for my electric project the US Fish and Wildlife Service said because you didn't find them **"We must** *assume*" they are there. This is the mentality of these people. I requested the USFWS representative come out to the site to see for herself if the possibility could exist. She ignored the request, preferring instead to sit in her Sacramento air conditioned office and do everything via email.

A few years ago the environmentalist movement in California tried to stop sport fishing. Their reasoning was that they thought the hooks hurt the little fishes mouths. I guess the frying pan doesn't hurt as much. Is this their real goal? To stop sport fishing? If you can't accomplish it one way, try another.

Another environmental news report said the developers of a housing tract were put on hold because they found a new breed of spiders. These spiders were so small that you could barely see them on the head of a pin. If there is one thing I can guarantee, spiders will live anywhere.

Now the environmentalists want to expand the CRLF habitat to include virtually almost all of California. It is time California put an end to this madness. It is time that California sued the Federal Government to remove the California Red Legged Frog, the California Yellow Legged Frog and the King

Garder Snake and other so called threatened and endangered species from the all controlling endangered/threatened species list. The California Red Legged Frog is a prime example of protectionism gone mad. It is time for clear thinking people to stand up and put a stop to this madness. Unfortunately the eco-nuts, the Center For Bio Diversity and the Earth Liberation Front, with support from Congress and the likes of House Speaker Nancy Pelosi, Senate Majority Leader Harry Reid, and (soon) with support from President-elect Obama, have discovered they can delay development and stop things like stocking fish in lakes, prevent logging because of the Spotted Owl and prohibit drilling in ANWR, through legislation. Unfortunately they have the money to do so.

Like most Californians I didn't think much about frogs until I got involved in a rural electrification project that has been significantly delayed due to the California Red Legged Frog. The proposal to expand the California Red Legged Frog habitat that will only make things worse. The cost to taxpayers in an all ready overburdened economy must stop. It seems like frogs are more important and valuable to the environment than human life or carbon footprint. It doesn't matter that I use 150 gallons of propane per month just to generate electricity on a solar energy system, only that I don't accidently disturb a frog.

Projects are delayed years due to environmental issues and at an extremely high cost to the taxpayer, the developer and ultimately to the purchaser. These projects are delayed, for surveys only to eventually allow the project's completion. This results only in delaying much needed energy and construction projects, does not stop development and does not protect any species. Taxpayers spent nine million dollars constructing a highway to nowhere to avoid a family of beavers, which by the way got ran over by traffic anyway. Then we are told because the project completed early the taxpayers saved three million. I could have relocated the beavers for a few hundred dollars and saved the taxpayers over eight million dollars. We have spent millions buying and rebuilding snake habitat, add more millions in fire suppression in over protected and over managed forests. California is bankrupt. America is bankrupt. Why? Because of failed environmental policies put in place by a primarily Democrat

Congress and also to avoid lawsuits by eco-terrorists like the Center for Bio Diversity.

As far as stocking farm grown fish in the lakes and the environmental position; they seem to think that introduced (stocked hatchery grown) fish are a threat to the California Red Legged Frog habitat but not natural fish. Who knew a trout grown in a fish hatchery had a different diet than brook trout! This is ridiculous.

Most animals added to the endangered or threatened species list are added due to the cute factor. The New Mexico Field Jumping Mouse along with Deer Mice and other rodents that carry the deadly Hanta Virus but they are cute so they are on the endangered species list. The only reason is these poor little mice are cute, as is the Polar Bear and baby Otters, deer, etc. I don't see anyone out there trying to get the Sidewinder a very rare species or the Pacific Diamondback added to the list. What about the poor little Ring Neck Red Belly snake?

To the environmentalist I assert that the mosquito is the mainstay of the California Red Legged Frog's diet and therefore should be protected as part of protecting the California Red Legged Frog habitat. I further assert that it is because of mosquito vectoring that the frog population has diminished due to the malathian used in vectoring. It is the mosquito vectoring that is the real cause of the decline on the number of (if there really is a decline) the California Red Legged Frog and therefore I want all mosquito vectoring stopped and the mosquito be added to the threatened species list. I further propose that because humans are a mainstay of the mosquito's diet that humans be added to the threatened species list. Sounds pretty ridiculous doesn't it? It makes as much sense as any of their proposals.

Not only are these environmental policies costing Californians millions, they are costing every other states millions of dollars in lost revenue from development. This cost millions in tax dollars for useless surveys and site assessments so somebody can do their collage thesis on these ridiculous projects. *These environmental issues are the main reason President-elect Obama's New-New Deal won't work.*

President-elect Obama says he will keep or create 2.5 million jobs. Now it has been revised to up now to 4 million. The emphasis should be on "keep." He supports infusing the economy with infrastructure spending but never having worked on anything but legislating, campaigning and community organizing, he has no concept of what it takes to get a project done. According to Carl Rove, Bush's Brain, only 26¢ per dollar on infrastructure spending goes into a project in the first year. The balance is usually spent in the seventh, eighth and ninth year. From my experience that is true but it might be more like the twentieth year. In 1988 the Federal Highway Department bought the right-of-way to widen FH 119. The environmental impact report was completed in 2001 and construction began in 2005. The nine kilometer section was completed in November 2007 and dedicated in June 2008. Twenty years after the right-of-way was purchased. I often wonder how many years the job was in the planning stage before the right-of-way was purchased.

Agencies that are involved in any construction project include the EPA, the US Fish and Wildlife Service, the Army Corp of Engineers, US Department of Agriculture, the Air Quality Management District, local Water District, Historical Preservation Society, Federal, State and local departments and executive orders, local tribes and environmentalists.

The reason President-elect Obama's New New Deal plan is deemed to failure is because he supports all of these extremist environmental views. So in order for his plans to come to fruition he would have to suspend all the environmental policies he supports.

Obama is an oxymoron in his thinking.

The Mortgage Meltdown

A friend told me he was voting for candidate Obama and said "I know you support the war." We don't support the war. We do support bringing the troupes home in victory, and explained to him that we didn't support the war. Then he came up with the Democratic rhetoric, "Are you better off today than you were eight years ago?" Well, at that time eight years would have put us into the Clinton Administration as did all the rhetoric. The question should have been, are you better off now than you were in 2006? And the answer would have been no. But in 2006 something happened that the Americans forget about. In 2006 the Democrats became the majority in both the House of Representatives and the Senate. For the first six years of the Bush administration, despite inheriting a recession, September 11th and involvement in two wars and multiple hurricanes, the country had six years of low unemployment and economic prosperity. So what happened? Sorry to have to say it but a Democratic Congress led by Senator Harry Reid and Congresswoman Nancy Pelosi, coupled with an environmental policy that is crippling our economy and has created much of the mess we are in.

Combine a moratorium on drilling, extremely high gas prices and bad environmental policies with bad economic policies like Mark to Market, and the Community Reinvestment Act add in groups like ACORN and you have the economic collapse of 2008.

In 1980, President Clinton repealed the Glass-Siegel Bank Regulation Act.

On September 10, 2003 Barney Franks, Democratic House Financial Services Committee Chairman representing the state of Massachusetts testified before Congress. I have copied the full text of Mr. Franks testimony because I think it is important to understanding how we got here. It recently was exposed that Barney Franks' lover was a executive at Fannie Mae. I don't care if the man is gay and don't care who he shares his bed with but don't do it on tax dollars. At the very minimum Mr. Franks should have recused himself.

And I now recognize the ranking member, the gentleman from Massachusetts, Mr. Frank.
Mr. Frank. Thank you, Mr. Chairman.

I appreciate hearing from the two Cabinet secretaries, but I would say at the outset that before we move on any legislation, I would hope we would have some additional hearings. And, in particular, I think it is important that the variety of groups in our country who care about housing be invited, because that is my major focus here, as it has been during my service on this committee. I want to begin by saying that I am glad to consider the legislation, but I do not think we are facing any kind of a crisis. That is, in my view, the two government sponsored enterprises we are talking about here, Fannie Mae and Freddie Mac, are not in a crisis. We have recently had an accounting problem with Freddie Mac that has led to people being dismissed, as appears to be appropriate. I do not think at this point there is a problem with a threat to the Treasury. I must say we have an interesting example of self-fulfilling prophecy. Some of the critics of Fannie Mae and Freddie Mac say that the problem is that the Federal Government is obligated to bail out people who might lose money in connection with them. I do not believe that we have any such obligation.

And as I said, it is a self-fulfilling prophecy by some people.

So let me make it clear, I am a strong supporter of the role that Fannie Mae and Freddie Mac play in housing, but nobody who invests in them should come looking to me for a nickel–nor anybody else in the Federal Government. And if investors take some comfort and want to lend them a little money and less interest rates, because they like this set of affiliations, good, because housing will benefit. But there is no guarantee, there is no explicit guarantee, there is no implicit guarantee, there is no wink-and-nod guarantee. Invest, and you are on your own.

Now, we have got a system that I think has worked very well to help housing. The high cost of housing is one of the great social bombs of this country. I would rank it second to the inadequacy of our health delivery system as a problem that afflicts many, many Americans. We have gotten recent reports about the difficulty here.

Fannie Mae and Freddie Mac have played a very useful role in helping make housing more affordable, both in general through leveraging the mortgage market, and in particular, they have a mission that this

Congress has given them in return for some of the arrangements which are of some benefit to them to focus on affordable housing, and that is what I am concerned about here. I believe that we, as the Federal Government, have probably done too little rather than too much to push them to meet the goals of affordable housing and to set reasonable goals. I worry frankly that there is a tension here. The more people, in my judgment, exaggerate a threat of safety and soundness, the more people conjure up the possibility of serious financial losses to the Treasury, which I do not see. I think we see entities that are fundamentally sound financially and withstand some of the disastrous scenarios. And even if there were a problem, the Federal Government doesn't bail them out. But the more pressure there is there, then the less I think we see in terms of affordable housing. I want Fannie Mae and Freddie Mac to continue as government sponsored enterprises with some beneficial arrangement with the Federal Government in return for which we get both the general lowering of housing costs and some specific attention to low-income housing. In particular, I am concerned right now that there has been~and it has been raised by

Fannie Mae, it has been raised by one of the rating agencies that have been critical of the Federal Home Loan Bank~manufactured housing.   Manufactured housing is a very important housing resource for low- and moderate-income people. You talk about increasing homeownership among low- and moderate-income people, and disproportionately, if you look at the increases in homeownership, it has come with their ability to get manufactured housing; and I do not want to see Fannie and Freddie pushed in the direction of being tougher on manufactured housing. And many of us will be in touch with Secretary Martinez to see how we can improve this.   I have talked to my colleagues in the Congressional Black Caucus, and the Blue Dogs. This is a very important and, I think, somewhat underrated form of housing. I think we now see pressure on it that is generated in part by exaggerated fears of a financial crisis.

So I am prepared to look at possibilities here, but in particular~and this is the major point I want to make; I saw this in the letter from the homebuilders~I do not want to see any lessening of our commitment to getting low-income housing.

And here is my concern: If you move the regulator to Treasury and you leave HUD with the mission, I am not sure that it isn't ``mission impossible,'' or at least implausible. What is HUD going to do, yell at them? I mean, if all the regulatory authority and all the clout is over in Treasury, what is left in HUD? And I noticed that the homebuilders raised that.

So my threshold question is, if you move this regulator to Treasury, if you bifurcate in terms of the Cabinet departments the responsibility for the low-income housing mission, including manufactured housing-- very important to me, as I said--and other forms of housing, if you bifurcate that, what real strength is there left behind the mission if most of the regulation and most of the teeth--I guess if you put all the teeth from Treasury, having HUD gum them into doing more low-income housing doesn't strike me as the ideal situation.

And that is why I say, Mr. Chairman, in closing, that as we proceed on this, I would hope we would have a day when groups, a range of groups that are concerned with housing, could specifically address that.

Thank you. – Barney Franks September 10, 2003 [2]

In 2006 John McCain added his support to Federal Housing Enterprise Regulatory Reform Act of 2005, S.190. Paraphrasing Barney Franks attitude, if it ain't broke don't fix it. But it was broke and we didn't fix it. Now we have the economic collapse of 2008, 2009 and beyond.

The numbers speak for themselves. As of December 27, 2008; at 8515 the Dow is down 390% from 1987 recession, 36% this year 2008, 3.5% this month (December) and 8% the last week of December 2008. Percentage wise it is the worst year since 1931. The S&P index is no better. It's at 873, down 288% from 1987, 40% for the year, 2.6 % for the month, and 1.79% for the week. NASDAQ has lost 325% of its 1987 value, 42% in 2008, .4% for the month and 2.2% for the week. Jobless numbers are the highest in 26 years but that doesn't account for the people who are underemployed or just simply gave up looking. 45% of recent

---

[2] 108th CONGRESS
1st SESSION
SEPTEMBER 10, 2003
Serial No. 108-51

home sales were in the foreclosure market. In 2008 only 18 out of 10800 banks failed. Only eighteen banks. These are the official numbers. The economists were asleep at the wheel and failed to recognize the true economic situation. They were about a year late on calling it a recession. Now they are hedging on deflation, the new buzz word for depression.

Congress throws tax dollars at what is rapidly becoming a wildfire with all the results of a fireman urinating over the side of the hill. So they throw more tax dollars into the flame.

You have the American Dream, a home of your own, or perhaps you want to build the American Dream. They told you that you could never loose on Real Estate. Guess what? You did. My house value has declined. The economy is in a recession. You have seen the government bailouts. What about me you ask. I am stretched to the max. I would like a government bailout. Wait long enough and you might get your wish. Barney Franks has said he wants to pay your mortgages. Testifying before congress Barney Franks likes to talk. He objects just to object. He appears to enjoy the sound of his own voice.

Most Americans didn't know the world was coming to an end until September 15, 2008 when Treasury Secretary Paulson with support from Federal Reserve Chairman Ben Bernanke, testified before Congress, presenting a three page request for seven hundred billion dollars ($700,000,000,000) in economic bailouts. He told Congress the world would come to an end if his Troubled Assets Recovery Package wasn't passed immediately. And the stock market plummeted. I wonder how much Paulson and Bernanke received for that. Was this another Pay-for-play issue? I have no proof of this. The thought just that keeps going through my head.

When Paulson speaks people listen. John McCain, who was at that time leading in the polls, suspended his campaign and returned to Washington to try to make a difference in an economic bailout plan that he didn't support. Many people believe this single act cost him the election. John McCain did what I believed a presidential candidate should do. Work for the people. Democrats instead of recognizing his commitment to the country used this as political fodder for their campaign ads and political jokes. Candidate Barrack Obama said call if you need me I'm too busy running for president. He did, however, return to Washington, without suspending his campaign, when he was called by President Bush.

Unable to come to an agreement on an economic bailout plan, and even though the world was coming to an end, Congress shut down and went on holiday. Rosh Hashanah, a Jewish holiday was more important than doing their jobs. They also took off for the Christmas break, Yom Kippur and Hanukkah. I guess most of our Congress must be deeply religious and committed to their faith. Where is their commitment to their jobs and the American people?

When Congress reconvened Treasury Secretary Paulson's request for $700,000,000,000 didn't satisfy Congress, they had to add an additional $120,000,000,000 in pork. In Senate hearings on the economic bailout Senate Majority Leader Harry Reid argued that taxpayers should pay for children's eyeglasses. Now I am sorry, I don't see how this qualifies as economic stimulus. Nor do I understand tax credits for rum importers, wool producers or the manufactures of wooden arrows for children. Frankly, I don't think children should play with arrows, guns, knives or any other weapon. But apparently Congress does.

A few other pork barrel spending Congress has approved include water free urinals, the Sparta Teapot Museum, olive fruit fly research, alternative uses for Tobacco, money to study the potential use of wood burning on the east coast, New York grape genetics and of course lobster biscuits for dogs. Now I love my dogs but I can't even afford to eat lobster much less afford to feed it to my dog. And who can forget the tax dollars spent on hearings regarding the use of steroids in sports? Did you know your tax dollars were also spent on box car derby racing in the capitol? Republican Congressman John Doolittle testified before the House of Representatives asking for removal of a moratorium on offshore drilling and then a Democrat sponsored a bill on Box Car Derby racing. I didn't catch his name I was more interested in drilling, but I did notice the D under it.

The worst part of the economic bailout and one that Congress approved is Secretary Paulson asked for what amounted to a blank check. He came to Congress with three pages of proposals, with unlimited power for himself. Congress added another 468 pages of pork but gave it to him. *No strings attached.* Now Congress wants to know where the money has been spent and why they are not getting accountability. Well, dah.

Now Congress is putting together an $850 billion dollar stimulus package up from $820 billion depending on what news report you listen to. This is called the American Recovery and Reinvestment Act of 2009. It includes new automobiles for Washington but not new cars for you.

We also have Mortgage Backed Securities to contend with. MBS as they are called is said by economists to be a worse problem coming down the pipeline than the mortgage meltdown. The Federal Reserved has identified four firms to manage $500 billion in tax dollars securing these toxic assets.

How did we get here? President-elect Obama, the public and David Axelrod want to blame the economic meltdown on the Bush administration. And there is enough blame to go around. A largely Democratic Congress passed an $820 billion dollar bailout. They keep calling it a $700 billion dollar bailout but Congress added $120 billion in pork spending which everybody wants to sweep under the rug. Of the $700 billion President-elect Obama asked President Bush to request the additional unspent $350 billion. This way he can add that to the Bush Blame Game. David Axelrod says there has been no transparency in the management of the first $350 billion and that Obama's $825 billion dollar stimulus package would create jobs. He goes on to say that "It's not that easy even for government" (to track the money). How can they fix the problem if they can't even track a mere $350 billion dollars? When pressed on job creation Axelrod says "We'll find out what the truth is." Shouldn't he know what the truth is? Now Obama and the Pelosi administration just passed another $850 billion dollar stimulus package. But it will get bigger. Only six Republican Congressmen voted for this albatross. I guess another $850 billion will be easier to track than the first $820 billion. The extra five billion will ensure that. That is a total of $1,640,000,000,000, one trillion six hundred forty million tax dollars. Axelrod goes on to tell George Stephanopoulos that (the economy is so bad) only government can fix the problem. Government created the problem so how can we expect government to fix the problem?

House Republican Leader John Boehner's response to the Obama economic stimulus package was simply "Oh, my God." He goes on to say that the Republicans in the House were not consulted before the package was presented to the House, a charge Axelrod denies.

Barrack Obama asked about the economy says "I think we can fix it." Think! At this point you better know. I have noticed when Obama speaks he often seems distracted. Like someone going through the motions while looking around, too busy and too disinterested to give the listeners his full attention.

In 1977 President Jimmy Carter supported and signed the Community Reinvestment Act. In 1995 Clinton with help from ACORN and Congress lowers borrower standards with Clinton's new version of the Community Reinvestment Act.

The economists want to blame the mortgage meltdown on Mark to Market. A fancy term that means your house value goes down if your neighbor's house value goes down. That means if you are a developer and you have just built a new housing development and one of the new owners defaults on the property and then the house is sold under the current market value your whole project just declined in value. Mark to Market is how your house is appraised when it is compared to recent sales in the area.

When you are a mortgage financial institute and are financing 1000 homes in the same area, all 1000 homes have just devalued. Banks and lending institutions borrow money against these values. If they suddenly loose 50% of value, then the bank's ability to borrow and lend is in jeopardy. You then have the current mortgage meltdown situation.

Mark to Market is also how neighborhoods were integrated with something called block busting. Block busting is where a person who is considered undesirable moves into the neighborhood to reduce house prices.

But it went way beyond Mark to Market. ACORN was heavily involved as were predatory lenders.

Housing prices escalated. Speculators bought houses to flip them. Environmental concerns added to home prices. Counties added permit requirements for house painting, air conditioning installation, shower replacement, water heater and stove replacements etc. Engineered septic tank became the requirement. Septic tanks which engineers have said may or may not work the way they think, added thousands of dollars to individual development. Then the green movement added more. A San Francisco 500 square foot studio went for over $1,000,000,000. Housing prices were artificially inflated by speculators. Introductory mortgage rates were as low as 2.3%. Teaser rates that sucked inexperienced and naive buyers into believing they could afford these properties. Predatory lenders and deceptive mortgage brokers told naive buyers that they could refinance once they were in their home. But without sufficient equities, when the collapse occurred there was no refinancing. Then their interest rates reset. People who were struggling collapsed under the weight of overpriced homes, high interest rates and high gas prices.

Companies like Bear Stearns and Lehman Brothers began to faultier like a deck of cards blown in the wind. With a too big to fail mentality Congress attempted to intercede. With no controls, no oversight and no strings. It doesn't work. Congress allocates more money throwing good after bad in a failed attempt to stabilize the

economy. Billions go to Merrill Lynch and
then to Bank of America to buy Merrill
Lynch. Bank of America still declares losses.
Like the $5,000,000,000 Waterford Crystal
ball slipping into the New Year, the economy
goes into a predictable slide. Round and
Round it goes. Where does it stop, nobody
knows.

To Congress I offer the following:

We have a lot of displace Americans who
have lost their homes to multiple hurricanes,
flooding, wildfires, mudslides etc. Currently
FEMA puts these people up in rented
apartments, hotel rooms and even cruise
ships. Why not take FEMA funds and buy
up some of these toxic assets, work with
Habitat for Humanity to refurbish them and
use them for evacuees. Then sell these
houses to the occupants in exchange for not
rebuilding in high risk areas. This would get
toxic assets off the books, give people a place
to live and the opportunity of home
ownership and spend funds are all ready
being spent. Take the insurance money and
use it to clean up and restore these areas.
Any excess insurance could go towards the
principal or if sufficient insurance to pay off
the principal the excess would go back to the
homeowner. The insurance used would be

the homeowners rebuilding portion and any insurance that covered the contents should go to the homeowner. The areas that flood and are destroyed on a routine basis are the areas we need to give back to the snakes and frogs, not producing farmland.

Even though President-elect Obama has indicated he wants to allow Bush's tax credit to expire in 2010, Nancy Pelosi says they are responsible "for the biggest increase in the budget deficit than any element you can name" and further that they have to "prove their wealth to me (her)." Nancy Pelosi has a very different take on the economic meltdown and blames the $35 million dollar Bush tax credits for the trillion dollar deficit spending that she and fellow Democrats are forcing down taxpayers throats in an attempt to stave off the economic mess they created.

Oil and Energy

John McCain said the mortgage meltdown was the match that lit the fire to the economic collapse but I disagree. I say the spark that lit the match was oil prices. I will tell you from experience most people will try everything to make their mortgage and keep their homes. Local rents are often about the same as their mortgage and most clear thinking people would rather not end up out in the street. This is just common sense. It is not a matter of being upside down on their mortgage, owing more than the house is worth, it is a matter of the cost of living, i.e. gas prices, food and medical costs exceeding the available income. It is impossible for a person to make their mortgage when they can't afford the price of milk for their children. Or more accurately they can't afford milk because every dime goes into the gas tank to get them back and forth to work. Once they lose their job, become disabled or even divorce they simply have no options. The increase in gas prices is particularly devastating to anyone who makes their living on the road like the independent owner operator truck driver. Even major trucking firms are reducing their hours and workforce. Farmers use not only large amounts of water but large amounts of fuel to harvest and transport their crops. This cost has to be passed on to the consumer. Increased insurance rates and added environmentally mandated equipment retrofits like the $25,000 per diesel truck retrofit have to be passed on. Every dime increased in operating expense to the farmer, the truck driver and even to the grocer has to be passed on to the consumer.

Why did gas prices get so high?

You can start with a moratorium on offshore drilling and nuclear power. Add in a mix of artificially inflated oil prices due to speculation and fear, OPEC reducing production, then an increased demand from developing countries, three major hurricanes in the Gulf, a concentration of refineries in the Gulf, and refineries that shut down for maintenance at the peak of the driving season, stir well and you have the recipe for economic disaster.

This was no accident and should have been easily predicted but nobody wanted to listen. Nancy Pelosi wanted to push oil exploration in areas that showed no likelihood of petroleum resources because the oil companies already owned the leases on the land. She wanted drilling in excess of fifty miles offshore. I guess she thinks most dinosaurs were aquatic animals. In other words Congress wanted oil companies to spend millions drilling dry wells simply to placate an ignorant Congress.

To add insult to injury while Americans are suffering and losing their jobs Congress received a raise. They voted in place an automatic raise so no matter how bad they were, how poor their performance, Congress would get an automatic raise. That way they don't look bad by voting on it in times of economic hardship. I think Congress' salary should be tied to performance. If you don't balance the budget, you don't get paid. The raise Congress got didn't amount to much. Only $4700 per year but that brought Nancy Pelosi salary to $217,400.

After billions of tax dollars spent on bailing out banks and lending institutions the same banks and lending institutions are refusing to disclose where the economic bailout package is being spent. Added to this the states came with hand out. Now the casinos in Los Vegas are saying their profits are down and they should be eligible for an economic bailout. The mayor of Los Vegas wants taxpayers to build a museum dedicated to Organized Crime. Doesn't the mob have enough money to build their own museum? Founder of Hustler Magazine, Larry Flint came with hand out. I guess with hard economic times the perverts can't spend as much money on pornography. That's one upside to the economic meltdown. We are passing an insurmountable debt to our Great-great-great grandchildren. We have artificially inflated a faltering economy. Maybe it is time to start over, let what's going to happen, happen and then just start over with a Fair Tax structure. How about no longer rewarding people who choose to increase the population with increasing tax credits but rather reward those who don't.

But in spite of hard economic times, in spite of budget deficits, just to cheer us up we spend millions on electricity for Christmas lights and trees wasting both energy and tax dollars. And anybody who sees it that way is supposed to have a war on Christmas. Has anybody ever heard of the First Amendment the Separation of Church and State? I don't mind the lights; I think they are beautiful; I just don't want taxpayers to pay for them. If citizens want to donate their money and time to pay for civic displays I don't have a problem. Just pay the electric bill.

Congress has approved more failed programs with no oversight. Billions are spent annually on a failed War on Drugs and Immigration policies. The ill make trips to Mexico and Canada to obtain prescription medication to treat their ills. Retirees retire to Mexico because it is cheaper to live but when the Mexicans come into the United States we greet them with contempt. Immigrants often are turned into immigration on payday. Female undocumented immigrants are often subjected to unwanted sexual advances and forced to consent to keep their jobs. Workers who are injured are simply deported even when the employer doesn't have Workman's Compensation insurance. In short the immigrant is often exploited when they come here to pick our vegetables and do the jobs Americans have traditionally turned down. Immigrants often pay into the system even when working illegally. Payments into a Social Security system that they will never receive benefits from. And what do the kind hearted Americans do? We build a wall. But only on the southern border. Didn't Regan say *"Mr. (Mikhail) Gorbechoff tear down this wall?"* and then we have the audacity to do the same. But as I said only on the southern border. The fact that most of the September 11th terrorists came in through Canada is virtually ignored. The only reason I can see for the disparity is they don't look as much like us as the Canadians do. We would rather isolate than educate. We need to work with Canada and Mexico. It is easier to protect a border when that border is separated by an ocean.

President-elect Obama received 75% of the Hispanic vote.

During the 2008 election the Democrats would compare John McCain to George W Bush saying that the policies Bush put in place with the economic bailout were socialists. Policies that Bush was forced to enact when Paulson told everybody the world was collapsing. Yet these same people refuse to believe Obama's policies are socialistic policies. I thought Obama's Change was supposed to be different but President-elect Obama's ideas seem to be an extension of what the media is calling failed Bush economic policies. A Democratic Congress held the purse strings and added $120 billion in pork but it is George W Bush's sole responsibility.

Obama's bailout is more of the same socialism that everybody wants to blame Bush for. These weren't just Bush's policies but rather a Democrat ran Congress's failed economic policies. Bush's legacy will be democracy for the Iraqi people. I don't support the WMDs use to justify the war, this was deceptive advertizing, but I believe we must come home in victory. We have a moral responsibility to see that the country is rebuilt and it has a functioning government before we leave.

We need to reduce our energy consumption not only through conservation but also through population control. We need to build the power plants that will bring us into the 21st century. Nuclear Power as well as hydroelectric, clean coal and anything else we can do to meet the needs of the people.

In Tennessee a sludge spill from a coal burning power plant burst through a holding pond. The EPA is showing high levels of arsenic and other heavy metals in the river. I would have a little more confidence if the EPA released previous water studies and took samples of the sludge for testing rather than just testing the water. First find contaminates in the sludge before you blame it. Don't assume all of the contaminates came from the sludge and not another source until you can prove it.

Now that Americans have conserved Congress wants to increase gas taxes. Not much just 18¢ a gallon. Their reasoning is because of the high gas prices people are driving less; therefore revenues are down so they need more money to repair the highways. Just more sleight of hand.

Bill O'Reilly where are you? You said any gas company that was helping the people you would support. Up until recently CITGO was doing just that. Recently they suspended heating oil assistance delivered to 400,000 households in 23 states through Citizen Energy. This was a program sponsored by Venezuela's President Hugo Chavez. It is said this program was to covet political favors. Compare this to a Congress who wants to increase the gas tax. Congress did this a few years ago too, but nobody was watching. Nobody paid attention.

Europe receives 25% of its natural gas from Russia. So what does Russia do? They shut off oil and gas to the Ukraine and uses energy as a weapon. With no heating oil, people freeze to death. Twenty five percent of all natural gas going to Europe goes

through the Ukraine. Is anybody surprised
oil and gas are being used for extortion?

Automobile Bailout

Perhaps a better solution than to bail out Detroit would be to give every American a new fuel efficient car. This would help every American plus keep Detroit working as well as get older polluters off the road. Don't need a new car, how about in five years. We could give American's new cars based upon a need priority system. It sounds better than giving cars to Congress and billions to industries that have shown little desire to make the changes necessary to compete in an international market. Granted the economic collapse has exacerbated the situation and Toyota has lost money for the first time in its history. Realize Detroit's problems began years ago. Congress has included new cars for themselves in the economic stimulus package, why not the people?

The 1973 oil embargo resulted in Americans lining up for gas on alternate days based upon odd or even license plate number and found Americans fighting at the gas pumps over gas. Automobiles with strange names like Datson and Toyota appeared on the market. Energy efficient tin boxes that rapidly took over the market. Detroit made the Cadillac, and other gas guzzling eight cylinder muscle cars. Americans sent a clear message to Detroit. We wanted inexpensive, fuel efficient transportation. We were willing to give up comfort and some safety to save money. Not satisfied and in an attempt to protect the consumer Congress imposed both Safety Standards and in 1975 CAFÉ (The Corporate Average Fuel Economy) Standards. Ironically CAFÉ standards made cars less safe in that in order to comply with these standards car manufactures had to remove weight. This meant using lighter materials. Then safety standards increased and more weight was added to the automobile in the form of airbags and other safety equipment. Do you see the paradox here? It's an infinite circle trying to comply with both the environmental and safety standards and still make a product that the consumer wants and can afford.

Detroit's solution was unveiled at the 2008 International Auto Show in San Francisco. Chrysler's new car is a muscle car. General Motors new Volt, news reports said it didn't even run. Yet it is slated to be on the market in 2010. It's no wonder Detroit's Automakers bleed $3 Billion dollars per month.

Now the Obama administration wants to add Cap and Trade which will further impact the industry.

A recent trip to my Toyota dealer confirmed my previous belief that hybrid cars did not pay for themselves. I have listed the most recent internet info from Toyota's website:

Camry Hybrid mpg city 33/34 hwy. suggested price $26,150

Camry (gas model) mpg city 21/31 hwy. suggested $19,145

Corolla (gas model) mpg city 26/35 hwy. suggested $15,350

Yaris (gas model) mpg city 29/36 hwy. suggested $12,205

Prius Hybrid mpg city 48/45 hwy. suggested price $22,000

Comparing Camry Gas model price savings to the hybrid there is a $7,005 upfront savings. At a 12 mile increase in mileage in the city and a 3 mile difference in highway miles how many years will it take you to recover the additional costs. What about carbon footprint. With the emission control equipment I would say emissions are about the same. For further reference the *$14,995 Ford Focus averages 35 mpg* both highway and city. Again there is a $7,005 up front savings compared to the Prius. The difference in mileage is 13 mpg highway and 10 mpg in town.

While the Prius gets the best mileage you can add to it the cost of replacement batteries when the fail and they will, but also add the cost to the environment of manufacturing and recycling these batteries and you will find the gas model is less polluting to the environment. Most people surveyed that have bought the hybrids did it because people think they are eco friendly.

Beyond Detroit's failure to recognize consumer preferences and I will say they do make some of the best automobiles in the world, Detroit has been constrain by the United Auto Workers.

Much of the union movement can be traced back to the 1905 Russian Revolution and Lenin when conflict occurred between the bourgeois and proletariat. The proletariat (poor people) thought the bourgeois (rich people) should "spread the wealth" and create jobs. So they organized.

Corrupt union leaders have existed throughout the labor movement as Robert F Kennedy documented in a book called the Enemy Within. The Teamsters Union under Jimmy Hoffa was repudiated to be controlled by the mob. Recent news articles in some local union papers still talk about mob activities.

Today the UAW with Ron Gettelfinger as the current UAW president has amassed over 1.2 billion in assets. With the mentality we are (again) too big to fail Ron Gettelfinger has refused to negotiate concessions in good faith that would help Detroit and potentially save the UAW.

The UAW has throughout its history spent money on a few bad ideas. They invested in a radio station that went bankrupt, the Black Lake Golf Course and Resort in Onaway, MI which has been reported to have lost $23 million over the last five years. They also bought an airline Pro Air which gave discounts to rank and file members and was subsequently closed for safety standards. The UAW also made a $9.75 million bid on a walled compound, La Mancha Resort in Palm Springs. In all fairness to Mr. Gettelfinger, not all of this was done under his watch, however from the average person's perspective it does sound like misappropriation and misuse of union funds. I wonder how many of the autoworkers flew on Pro Air, or how many played golf and vacationed at Black Lake and other resorts. I doubt that many did. The UAW successfully negotiated and got workers paid for not working in something called the Job Bank. No wonder Detroit is hemorrhaging $3 Billion per month. They are now asking for a Trillion Dollar Bailout package for the auto industry above and beyond the original bailout.

But the unions did do some good. Competitive wages and forty hour work weeks are the result of the labor movement. Also lunch and bathroom breaks. The United Farm Workers brought water and shade as well as competitive wages to the farm worker.

The Democrats including President-elect Obama are in support of the Employee Free Choice Act, otherwise known as Card Check. They say this will help workers and increase unionization. Guess what, this only takes away the secret vote. A few years ago I witnessed the unionization of a grocery store in Mariposa, California and I will tell you if Congress passes the Employee Free Choice Act it will result in Union Busting. People who do support unionization will fear retribution from management and retaliation from other workers who don't support unionization.

We all ready have Caucus in many states in preliminary elections. This disenfranchises the shift worker, the senior and the disabled. The Democrats refuse to go to secret ballot in these states. My brother-in-law went to the caucus in Colorado Springs; he said it was so disorganized he left without voting. Is this what they wanted? How long will it be before Congress tries to take away your secret ballot?

It's not that farfetched.

Whose Air is it Anyway?

The local television news station announces a Spare the Air Day. Nothing new, it happens all the time. I don't drive to town often but on this day I do. I notice the smoke. Not from the wood stoves but from slash burning. Windblown smoke from rice fields permeates the air. Piles of brush burning to clean up yards, hillsides and construction sites. Yet the homeowner is told not to use his woodstove to heat his home. A woman in Chico on the news, states that although she loves her wood stove she has given it up because she knows the smoke bothers her neighbor. Yet, Congress appropriates funding to study the potential for increased wood burning on the east coast. It took less than a year to abandon that idea saying the pollution carbon footprint would be too great.

The 2008 wildfires began with over 2000 lightning strikes and soon spread to over 700 wildfires. Then spread to over 2000 wildfires. Many of the fires were in remote locations which made firefighting difficult. Budgetary constraints prevented more from being done until as Congressman Wally Herger put it, enough acres have burned to apply for Federal Aid. In some cases people remained evacuated from their homes for over a month. More fires broke out, some from burning embers, some from lightning and others from arson or carelessness. One fire in Montecito, California started when collage students started a bonfire. They thought they put it out and left. The winds picked up and it burned out of control. Millionaires and homeless alike lost their places of residence as did deer population and other wildlife including the protected threatened endangered California Red Legged Frog. Fire doesn't distinguish between threatened habitat and anything else. The smoke and pollution blanked the state of California from Oregon to Mexico. There was no place to escape from the choking smoke. The sun shone bright red, if you could see it at all. In many places the smoke was so thick visibility was reduced to ten to twenty feet.

At the same time California passes an anti-smoking law that prevents people from smoking in their apartments or around their children in their own cars. Anti-smokers blame all respiratory problems on smoking.

Truck drivers have been ordered to retrofit diesel trucks to reduce pollution at a cost of $25,000 per vehicle. But we still allow slash burning on no burn days.

Candidate Obama says he supports Clean Coal technology while stating that any energy company that wants to build an electric plant using coal could do it but he would bankrupt them with the fines they would have to pay under his Cap and Trade Legislation, while at the same time saying "there is no such thing as Clean Coal Technology." If you think you are confused . . .

China on the other hand is building one coal powered plant per week for seven years. That is 364 green house gas spewing electric generation facilities. Not using clean coal technology but standard coal burning power plants. At the same time Americans are expected to comply with emission standards and support the Chinese economy by purchasing contaminated products because we owe the Chinese $500,000,000,000 (that's $500 Billion dollars).

When did we start borrowing so much money from the Chinese? A government that has no morality when it comes to human rights. A country that until just a few years ago we had a trade embargo against. A Communist county.

Have we forgotten about June 4, 1989 at Tiananmen Square? I remember watching as a young Chinese activist was run over by a military tank on live television. A tank provided by Russia.

Now we see Chinese children die from contaminated milk, people sickened worldwide by contaminated products made from contaminated milk, Americans die from contaminated Heparin and other pharmaceuticals that come out of China. We import, sell and then recall products from China that are contaminated with lead or products with small magnets or small breakable parts that are responsible for choking hazards in children. We participate in the Olympics Games whose opening ceremonies are held at the same Tiananmen Square where the man was killed, like nothing ever happened. The pomp and circumstance a stark contrast to the squalor hidden just a few feet from view. Camouflaged with hastily built facades. The air quality so bad the Olympic Committee contemplated cancelling some of the events. The bay turned green with algae that had to be scooped up in order to be able to have the rowing contests. It makes you wonder how contaminated the Chinese landscape is.

More than that, what about the women who work in many of the factories painting lead faces on dolls that are slated to be shipped to America? What of their health? What about their children? Of which they can only have one. What if your only child were to be born with lead poisoning or preventable birth defects? Who is looking out for these poor souls? Certainly not the American consumer.

I pick up an Native American art piece. It's labeled "Made in China" but is obviously made to look Native American (or African) in origin. These products are being sold at the military B-X. I make a conscious effort not to buy Chinese products. I read food labels and furniture labels. It is impossible to boycott as these products are all Made in China.

Free Trade and NAFTA

During the Primaries candidate Obama said he would renegotiate NAFTA. Just the threat of renegotiating NAFTA as Obama suggested during these debates, disenfranchises the Canadian and Mexican government. He opposes Free Trade with Colombia one of our few South American Allies.

Look at his Cap and Trade Legislation which Barbara Boxer says she will introduce in January. Legislation which in candidate Obama's own words will bankrupt the coal industry and cause our utilities to "skyrocket." We need to prevent this. We need to overturn the NEPA the Environmental Species Protection Act and anything else that is controlling development under protectionism mentality. I am just amazed at how uninformed the voters were when they voted Nancy Pelosi, Harry Reid, and all the other eco-terrorists back in office and worse of all they put one in the White House.

Even though Lady Liberty stands in the New York harbor, opened arms we have turned our back on our Mexican neighbors, building instead a wall to keep them out. At the same time Americans migrate to Mexico to live out their golden years under the Mexican sun. President-elect Obama nominates Arizona Gov. Janet Napolitano to head the Department of Homeland Security. To her credit she supports immigration but acting in combination with New Mexico Gov. Bill Richardson under the guise of drug suppression, helped get the funding to build the Great Wall of Mexico. There is just one issue here, Janet Napolitano says she doesn't support the wall.

Opponents of NAFTA have said it sends jobs to Mexico and Canada. When I go to the store I read the labels. You can't find a product that says Made in Mexico or Canada if you wanted to. I bought a sofa and when it was delivered I discovered to my dismay that it said "Made in China."

In the mean time Mexican immigrants contribute to the economy in many misunderstood ways. They take jobs from Americans. I have picked beans. I don't know too many Americans that are willing to do the jobs the Mexican immigrants do. They often pay into Social Security even through false IDs. Social Security that they will never receive benefits from. Yes, they may attend schools and receive medical benefits. Isn't it better to treat their illness rather than expose Americans to untold diseases? Just a thought.

Star Gazing
The Kennedy Legacy

More like Hollywood royalty than a potential candidate for US Senate, Caroline Kennedy drives into New York, assuming she is the presumptive Hillary Clinton replacement for New York Senator. She does this in a foreign made automobile. This while Detroit is begging at the heels of Congress. A major faux pas for any politician in this political and economic climate. After an interview with the press where she basically didn't answer any questions, she drives out of New York. In a Jeep.

The question has to be why would a woman who has never expressed any interests in politics be suddenly interested let alone be considered for a Senate seat? Has our star gazing so blinded us that we have forgotten what democracy is all about? How could a totally inexperienced candidate be considered the presumptive replacement? The only reason is name recognition and the Kennedy Legacy.

Dubbed Camelot; the Kennedy Administration was far different than that which has been portrayed by history and the media. Patriarch Joseph P Kennedy (Sr.) in 1938 was an avid Hitler supporter anti-Semite who amassed the family fortune as a bootlegger. Favorite son, Joseph P Kennedy Jr. died during a bombing raid in during WWII in 1944. Next in line was John F Kennedy. Elected amidst rumors of ballot stuffing and voter intimidation, a charismatic speaker John F Kennedy, a Catholic was at that time the youngest person elected to the White House. "Not the Chosen One" but the elected one, John F Kennedy brought us to the brink of nuclear war in a widely forgotten incident called the Cuban Missile Crisis. Kennedy promised to provide military support to Cuban Rebels at the Bay of Pigs. Rebels who wanted to overthrow Fidel Castro. Kennedy didn't bother to notify the rebels he had withdrawn his military support. Most of the rebels died at the Bay of Pigs. It is rumored John F Kennedy sent aids to purchase all the Cuban Cigars in Washington D.C., before he announced the Kennedy forced embargo on Cuba that is still in existence today.

At the time Jacqueline Kennedy was considered the most desirable, beautiful woman in the world. Conspicuously absent from Jack Kennedy's birthday party, soft spoken Jackie Kennedy refused to attend. Jack Kennedy's said to be mistress Marilyn Monroe sang a somewhat suggestive version of happy birthday.

Like they say ultimate power corrupts ultimately as we continually see as our politicians are caught in the wrong bed or bath stall. We act like this is new, but the only new thing is the media is actually reporting on it. Rumors swirled around the Kennedy administration. Even the media released the rumors as fact. That is until JFK was assassinated. Then he became a martyr. Almost God like in his standings. The media, with a little help from the Kennedy worshipers rewrote history. I lived it. I remember it. Subsequent reports have revealed a man who was a womanizer and addicted to pain medication.

Caroline Kennedy extols her qualifications as "a mother, a lawyer and an author." And besides she has work on education issues. She said she supported Barack Obama because he inspired her the way people told her that her father inspired them. But the nation was as divided in the Kennedy Administration as it is currently. Kennedy was relatively inexperienced president. He was popular with the same type of people who supported President-elect Obama but unpopular with others, like my father. So I didn't grow up worshiping the Kennedy Clan. I remember that time as being a very frightening time. A time of Duck and Cover. Now that was idiotic even to a seven year old child. History has treated Jack Kennedy, not with perspective and reality but with the rose colored glasses of those who worship martyrdom.

Obama likes to compare himself to Kennedy. And King. And also Lincoln. Obama is obsessed with Lincoln. Lincoln lived in a very different world than we do. The single common thread is one that nobody wants to talk about and that is that all three were assassinated. All three were martyrs. Let me public state that I don't want anything to happen to President-elect Obama. I hope he is a good president. I doubt that he will be based upon his own policies. But I can hope. The reality is the political chain of command. If something did happen to President Obama the nation would be in real trouble. The chain of command would put Joe Biden as President, Commander and Chief and Nancy Pelosi as Vice President. Nobody wants that. Nancy Pelosi is the most extreme environmentalist and would do anything "to save the planet" including bankrupting the American worker, the automotive industry and the electric industry. She sits on her throne like a queen, ruling from the House of Representatives. Taking makeup tips from her Castro Street "girlfriends" I will say she does remind me of a queen, a drag queen. Sorry to insult you boys.

Getting back to Caroline Kennedy. She is just plain inexperienced. She is trying to capitalize of the "I am one of you" grassroots mentality that came out of the Republican Campaign. The difference is that Sarah Palin has executive experience. More than any of the other candidates did but the voters rejected her. The voters said they would rather have inexperience and change. I say keep the change, I want the dollars. Especially when that change means taking the country from capitalism to socialism. When choosing any professional, from politician to a doctor, a Realtor to contractor, I want experience. Not political rhetoric and certainly not political name reorganization.

Caroline Kennedy has found disfavor with some Democrats and some in the media alike by avoiding the media and answering only eleven questions. She comes across with an air of entitlement. She avoids the media and refusals to disclose her financial information. Interestingly she said she will release the information *when* she is appointed. Not if but when. What does she have to hide? Even Bill Clinton has released his somewhat dubious contributions to his "library." Is "library" a euphemism for laundry?

Here is an interesting fact, Senator Hillary Clinton could have been elected to the highest office in the land but she has to disclose financial records and be confirmed before she can be appointed Secretary of State. President Bill Clinton's contributors to his foundation include the Kingdom of Saudi Arabia and other foreign governments who gave donations exceeding $46 million, while corporate donors included the Blackwater security firm donated tens of thousands of dollars.[3] They also received tens of thousands of dollars from Alavi Foundation an Iranian charity two days after its partner New York-based ASSA Corp. was labeled a terrorist organization by the Treasury Department. The New York

---

3

http://www.clintonfoundation.org/contributors/pages/page_1.html

Southern District's U.S. Attorney seized and forfeited assets owned by New York-based ASSA Corp. and indicted the president of the Alavi Foundation, Farshid Jahedi, on a charge of obstruction of justice.

During confirmation hearings Senator Clinton, Secretary of State Nominee tells Congress "I think that the way this is hammered out is probably as close as we can get to doing something that is so unprecedented that there is no formula for it." In other words don't ask me and I won't tell you.

Former Presidential candidate John Edwards admitted his infidelity while his wife was going through chemo treatments. Come to think about it Joe the Plumber was better vetted than the presidential candidates. Perhaps we need to do a better job of vetting our candidates long before they are elected.

Let's look at New York politics for a minute. Elliott Spitzer a Republican resigned in disgrace after an extramarital affair. The Lieutenant Governor is the next in line of secession. So Lieutenant Governor Patterson is sworn in. After the swearing in ceremony voters are treated to a confession and information regarding Democrat Lieutenant Governor Patterson's multiple infidelity and previous drug use only. But only after he ascends to Governor. There are no calls for him to resign. Why? Republicans are held to a higher standard. The Democrats are Liberal in their thinking and support your right to free speech, as long as you agree with them that is. Another example of Democratic double Standards came when Joe Lieberman, an Independent, supported John McCain because he believed John McCain was the best candidate for presidency. After the November election former Democratic Vice-presidential candidate Geraldine Ferraro said "Of course Joe Lieberman should be punished for not supporting the party" and then a few days later when asked said she will vote for Michael Bloomberg, a Republican, for Mayor of New York because he is doing a good job. Wasn't that what Joe Lieberman thought of John McCain? The Republicans are considered the party of Conservative Moral Values and fiscal responsibility. The Democrats are considered the liberal the open minded anything goes party. The Democratic Party brings out the stars in Hollywood. Now we are supposed to take political advice from actors, musicians and drug addicts.

"The monarch is the last person in his kingdom who yields to the progress of philanthropy and civilization."

~Thomas Jefferson to John Jay, 1788

Smoke and Mirrors

I wrote Bill Clinton regarding my struggles with solar energy asking for support for my grant application. He wrote me back and thanked me for my commitment to solar energy. I wrote him back and thanked him for his autograph. I told him that he obviously did not read my letter because if he had he would have come to a totally different conclusion. It's not that I am against solar. I'm not. What I am against is the lies the government has been selling. When I wrote Exposed; the Solar Energy Con I documented the fraud that is perpetrated in the name of green energy. But it goes way beyond Solar Energy.

We believe the scientists know what they are talking about. That's the problem, we believe. Like lambs being let to slaughter the environments movement has become a religion. Kool-Aid drinkers reminiscent of Jonestown. The scientists say there is global warming. So there must be, right? Wrong. Other scientist are just as sure that in the last 18 months the global temperature has actually decreased. The lower Pacific Ocean temperatures have produced an abundance of plant and animal life. Or we have a dire salmon and crab yield. No two scientists agree. When my mother was a child, in the early twentieth century, the scientist said smog was caused by pine trees. We do know that pine needles are acidic, but producing smog? Some scientists are saying we have more to worry from global cooling than we ever did from global warming? Russian scientists are saying we are entering 11,000 years of global cooling. They say we are actually entering an ice age. Who knows, we may be, wanting, needing and trying to generate a carbon footprint in the very near future.

Does anybody remember the hole in the Ozone layer? They said all the ozone was going into outer space. Now they tell us the Ozone count is too high and people with respiratory problems should stay inside.

So who do you believe? Start believing in yourself. Start using common sense and good judgment. Look at the facts and decide for yourself.

Speaker of the House, Democrat Nancy Pelosi is one of the worst airheaded eco-nut, deer caught in the headlights, Kool-Aid drinking eco-terrorists in the nation. She is the worst kind. She's a believer. Or not. The problem with Nancy Pelosi and what makes her so dangerous is she has the power to shut down the House of Representatives and did so. When interviewed by George Stephanopoulos she was asked why she shut down Congress and would not allow an up or down vote on offshore drilling. Republicans stayed in Washington and tried to get her to reconvene Congress. She was on her book tour and was flying around the country in her private taxpayer supplied Boeing 757 jet. She looked at the camera with that same deer caught in the headlight stare of the Kool Aid drinkers and without a clue said "Because we have a planet to save." She doesn't seem to have the same attitude toward her jet that she does toward saving the planet or Detroit's private jets. It's the constant double standard "do as I say, not as I do" mentality of the environmental movement. If Nancy Pelosi wants to claim environmentalist status then she should retire her Boeing 757 and fly commercial like everybody else does. She could take a few pointers from Ed Bagley Jr. He really does live the environmental lifestyle. Personally, if I was his wife I would divorce him.

Most environmentalists sit comfortably in their air conditioned offices, or homes, sipping lattés while watching their plasma

TVs, blogging on their computer about how we are destroying our environment. They tell you what **you should do**. But they don't seem to apply the same standards to their own lives. Just like President-elect Obama not being able to survive for a few hours without electricity on the island of Hawaii. I don't suppose he has ever heard of candles? Maybe Michelle would have liked a nice romantic evening?

Senator Ted Kennedy supports wind generators as long as it doesn't obscure his view when he is sailing.

Mr. Chicken Little Al Gore also flies around in his private jet, earning millions in speaking engagements on global warming. He recently installed some solar panels on his private yaught. Of course most of us don't have private jets or private yaughts to install over priced inefficient solar panels on.

Candidate Obama supports clean coal technology and then candidate Obama says clean coal technology doesn't exist. He also supports nuclear energy "As long as we can find a way to dispose" of the spent material. We have been safely storing nuclear waste for over fifty years. We also use spent uranium to dip weapons in. Weapons that

contaminate our enemy's environment.
Senator Feinstein supports this practice.

The Democratic portion of Congress
wants all offshore drilling to be in excess of
fifty miles offshore. Last I heard most
dinosaurs were not aquatic animals. They
didn't die fifty miles offshore. They died on
land and close to land. The concern seems
to be oil spills, yet mother nature spills more
oil per year than humans have spilled in the
years that we have been drilling.

ANWR, the holy grail of the
environmental movement is a section of
isolated frozen tundra that virtually nobody
has ever seen. It potentially holds more oil
than the Middle East, but the
environmentalist are committed to protecting
this piece of dry ice. If you have never seen
pictures of ANWR, the Arctic National
Wildlife Refuge, just look at some of them
on the internet, particularly of the area they
want to drill. Even the Polar Bear doesn't
live there, yet the environmentalist goal is to
protect ANWR for the Polar Bear all the
while making money on their speaking
engagements, surveys, studies, organizations
etc.

Here is the cute factor at work again.
Cute and cuddly white the Polar Bear has

been protected into endangerment. Recent studies say the Polar Bears population is at the highest it has ever been but other studies are now saying there isn't enough food for the Polar Bear. So man's intervention has caused overpopulation. Mother Nature has a way of balancing things out. After all, this planet has been around a lot longer than mankind. We are pretty arrogant of a species aren't we? We think we are the only life form in millions of universes and we think we can control the climate.

Photographs along the Alaskan Pipeline show a Polar Bear walking along the pipeline. They show Caribou nesting along the pipeline. The Alaskan Pipeline not only provides energy and jobs it provides warmth and shelter to the wildlife in an otherwise inhospitable wilderness. In short, the wildlife love it and it benefits the wildlife. The pipeline has been a win win situating for mankind and nature.

So then why don't the environmentalists want us to drill here? They say the environment; I say there is a more sinister more tangible reason. Follow the money trail. Nancy Pelosi is rumored to be heavily invested in Compressed Natural Gas.

What is CN?. My friend has family in Ohio where they use CNG so through his family he has some experience. He explained to me that it takes overnight to compress the gas and fill the tank on one of these wonder cars. The mileage range is about forty miles. I couldn't even get to the grocery store and back within forty miles. Beyond that how could the average commuter get to work and back on that distance limitation? California's Democrat ran Congress wants to tie development to carbon footprint so this seems to fit into their plan. Tell me on that mileage limitation, how could the trucker deliver his product?

One company recently built an electric car dealership in Chico, California. The owner proudly announced that the cars could go an average of forty miles without recharging. I guess forty miles is the goal or the gold standard of the environmental movement.

There is however a new Chinese car company called BYD. Their new plug in hybrid will get about 60 miles on a 7 hour charge. What will happen when we have power failures on the utility grid as we always do and they can't plug their cars in? Did anybody think about brown outs and black outs? How will you charge your car when the electricity goes out? I guess, you just stay home. Oh, I forgot to mention it's a hybrid; it has a small gas engine. Forget going to work unless you have a fossil fuel automobile for back up. How is that a savings? You have to have two or more cars. The BYD website says the car goes 300 km per charge and the batteries last about 2000 charges or 600,000 km. or 186,411 miles. If you believe that I have a bridge to sell you. Do the math and you will realize that if you drive and charge your batteries every day you will have to replace your batteries in about 5 ½ years. Experience proves batteries degrade with use. A battery that might last 60 miles between charges when new may only produce 50 miles after the first year and 40 miles after the second year. My Dyno batteries that I run my house on have failed after less than two and one half years. One failed in less than nine months, the second, just over a year. Of course the manufacturer has excuses and won't replace them. The previous batteries, Trojan were supposed to last 10 years but they failed after five. This is the downside of any alternative energy system. Batteries have to be replaced and recycled or they are an environmental contaminate often dumped in creeks and streams by the same so called environmentalists that are promoting solar and alternative energy. It takes electricity to manufacture batteries. Any hybrid and alternative energy system that uses batteries amounts to nothing more than a feel good alternative that doesn't benefit the environment.

It should be noted that again this BYD automobile is a hybrid; it is augmented with a small fossil fuel engine. Studies of hybrid cars have shown that most people buy them because it makes them feel like they are helping the environment. One report says a Hummer actually has a lower carbon footprint than the Prius.

Recently in California, and remember how California goes so goes the nation, the State Legislature announced they were going to introduce legislation that *Tied Development to Carbon Footprint.* So now Congress is telling people where they can or can't live due to supposedly carbon emissions. There goes your dream of retiring to the mountains.

So let's look a little further at CNG. T Boone Pickens was interviewed regarding his planned CNG and wind farm generating facilities. When asked why he was scaling back his plans he told Bill O'Reilly since oil prices had dropped it wasn't economical. And besides, in this economy, even he couldn't get financing. If T Boone Pickens, one of the wealthiest people in the world, can't get financing, then who can? But more than that if his plans are so great for the environment, why doesn't Nancy Pelosi and Al Gore put their money where their mouths are and help him out? Is it possible it's not the environment that they are protecting but rather their pocket book?

I am for an "all of the above" approach to energy. But without an infrastructure to deliver and refuel these alternative energy cars and without batteries that will deliver a reasonable distance we can build all the electric cars and CNG cars we want and you won't be able to drive them. If we want alternative energy vehicles we must first build the infrastructure. But, wait a minute, before we can build an infrastructure we must first complete years of environmental impact studies, California Red Legged Frog surveys, historical preservation studies etc. And by the time we get these things done we will be living in wickiups and teepees.

The environmental movement supports renewable energy and even requires a percentage of each state's electricity come from renewable energy. They seem to forget that hydroelectric is the cleanest and one of the most reliable renewable energies available. But they don't want to include hydroelectric in the count. Bambi is more important to these protectionists.

Yes we need to develop renewable energy, but we also need a way to keep trucks running along the highways. And CNG and electric vehicles won't do it. We need a viable source of energy, a bridge as it has been labeled, until we can develop energy solutions that work and are competitively priced.

Nobody should go bankrupt paying their energy bill. We need to drill ANWR and offshore and every other place that has a potential for energy. Recent surveys say 75% of Americans favor drilling offshore and in ANWR but our government, headed by the environmental protectionist movement won't listen. And the Republicans no longer have the majority.

> *"The generation which commences a revolution rarely complete it. Habituated from their infancy to passive submission of body and mind to their kings and priests,*

they are not qualified when called on to think and provide for themselves; and their inexperience, their ignorance and bigotry make them instruments often in the hands of the Bonapartes and Iturbides to defeat their own rights and purposes."

~Thomas Jefferson to John Adams, 1823

Defense and Religion

The founders of this great nation knew what they were doing when they added the First Amendment to the Constitution. This amendment guarantees the Separation of Church and State and also Free Speech. An amendment, an afterthought, the forefathers, mostly Free Masons, realized that in order to promote free thought the government could not tell its citizens how to worship or what they could or could not say. Yet even now the government is doing just that. In subtle ways. In God We Trust emblazons our money. We begin Congress with a prayer. Testify in court and you swear to God on a bible. I have often wondered if that would exempt an Atheist from telling the truth. We close government buildings for Christmas and even shut down Congress for Jewish holidays. We have Easter Egg rolls at the White House and give tax breaks to every church and religious institution. Even churches that preach hate and bigotry. However, if you use certain words you can be charged with a hate crime. ***Where is the freedom of speech here?***

We force convicted criminals to undergo behavior modification through faith based three step programs. In Florida after a friend got in minor trouble he revealed the probation department is administered through the Salvation Army. Who knew?

So where is the separation of church and state?

I don't want a zealot in the White House no matter what religion he claims. "W" or the Decider, as he is now called decided to use cowboy diplomacy and put out a wanted poster saying that Usama Bin Laden was wanted dead or alive. He built a deck of cards with his Al-Queda terrorist most wanted list. He just went looking in the wrong place. He took us on a diversionary road when he told us Saddam Hussein had weapons of mass destruction. Having worked in the aerospace industry where I went through bi-annual security briefings I believed him and supported the war as did 85% of all Americans. George W Bush had the highest rating of all presidents. Who would think he would close his presidency with the worst rating ever. Just slightly better than the Congress the American voter just reelected. The news reports that came out regarding the 9/11 Commission reported that Colin Powel presented nine year old evidence as current. This is my big beef with

Bush but also with Colin Powell. In all fairness to Bush, Saddam Hussein said before he was executed that he wanted the world to believe he still did have WMDs. That was pretty stupid of him. I blame the Iraq war on Saddam Hussein's arrogance.

My biggest problem with Bush is that he drew a line in the sand and effectively turned the Iraq War into a Religious War when he said "God is on our side." I would put money that the other side believes Ala (their name for God) is on their side too. When you make a declaration of moral high ground based upon your perception of God you better be right because you have the ultimate reason to keep on fighting. Right or wrong. And they have the ultimate reason to keep fighting too. After all, if you can't live free, in your homeland, and practice your own religion and you are going to die, you might as well die as a martyr. This makes perfect sense to anyone with strong religious beliefs. And scares the hell out of anyone with an ounce common sense.

The Sunnis bombed the holy shrine of the Shiites, the Golden Mosque in Samarra north of Bagdad. What does President George W Bush do? He promised the Iraqi people the United States Government would help them rebuild the mosque. Now regardless of the war in Iraq the possibility exists that the Sunnis may have bombed this mosque because there exists a civil war within the country. More than that, the United States did not bomb this building so why should American tax dollars be committed to reconstruction? If the United States or its allies would have inadvertently targeted the mosque during a bombing raid or a missile attack I would have no problem with helping to rebuild. I believe we have a moral obligation to reconstruct what we destroyed but we can no longer afford to be the world's piggy bank; we are not responsible to rebuild or finance the rebuilding of what everybody else tears down.

Bush said he looked into Putin's eyes and saw his soul. He must have been looking through rose colored glasses or through the mind fog of Alzheimer's or pharmaceuticals because Putin has revealed his true soul. After a shooting at a nursery school in Russia Putin suspended the 2004 elections saying it was too tumultuous of a time to change leaders. He then handpicked his successor and is trying to revise the Russian Constitution to allow him to serve as Russian president again.

During the 2008 election Russia invaded Georgia and told us we could not put defense missiles in Poland or sponsor Ukraine or Georgia into the United Nations. At the same time Peter the Great, a nuclear warship with armed nuclear weapons performed military exercises off Venezuela, with the approval and assistance of Hugo Chavez. On route home they made a stop off to visit Fidel and Raul Castro. Just off the Florida coastline. This was reminiscent of the Cuban Missile Crisis. As far as the media was concerned no big deal. The news media preferred to tell you about Sarah Palin's wardrobe and the Obama girl's choice for White House dog.

President-elect Obama's defense plans include *change* all right. He wants to form a *civilian paramilitary organization* because the civilian police can't adequately protect Americans. That sounds just a little bit too much like KGB or SS to me. Obama said he wants direct talks with Cuban, Iranian, Syrian and Hamas leaders. During the election he said he would talk with these leaders unconditional but he has since backed off on that position a little. President-elect Obama did receive telegrams of congratulations for winning the election from many of these leaders including Hugo Chavez and Hamas. It doesn't give me a warm fuzzy feeling when my nation's enemies support the president elect. On the other hand we have Ayman al-Zawahiri, Al-Qaeda's second in command, calling President-elect Obama a *""House Negro" (a Malcolm X coined term) who "claims" to be a Christian just to get elected. This is an apparent reference to Barack Obama abandoning his father's religion."*

Another President-elect Obama plan that bothers me is his desire to eliminate Strategic Air Defense. He has also expressed a desire and need to increase troop enlistment. At the same time he wants to cut defense spending putting our troupes in harm's way without sufficient armaments or equipment. Right now we have an all volunteer military. In order to achieve the objective of cutting military spending and increase enlistment, enlistment incentives would have to be eliminated. No matter how you add up the numbers the only way you can accomplish his goals is to institute the draft. If American wants to remain the world's super power that is. Presuming we do.

Obama has said that Americans will save billions after he withdraws from Iraq. What he doesn't tell you is that the money will be redirected to escalate the war in Afghanistan. Thirty thousand more troupes have been ordered to Afghanistan.

Defense Secretary Robert Gates says this fiscal year (October 1, 2008 to September 30, 2009) the U.S. military will need an additional $69.7 billion to continue operations in Iraq and Afghanistan. Above and beyond the Congress approved $65.9 billion already allocated. The 2010 budget proposal comes with a new five-year plan that would increase spending by a mere $450 billion. At a time when we are withdrawing from Iraq. This is war funding for Afghanistan. You can add to this the $700 million taxpayer built US embassy which recently opened in Iraq that includes movie theaters and shopping. An embassy city that is larger than the Vatican. Again at taxpayer's expense.

Since the election we have seen the bombing in Mumbai, India and the Israel/Palestinian conflict in Gaza. On top of the Russian invasion of Georgia during the election. This is the world situation President-elect Obama is inheriting.

The world is condemning Israel for its "Disproportionate Response" after the

Palestinians launched over 3000 rockets into Israel in the last year, including over 100 during the six month cease fire. In the last eight years they have launched over ten thousand rockets into Israel. And the world is condemning Israel for its "Disproportionate Response." Excuse me? The PLO, a terrorist organization, supported Hamas. The Palestinians elected Hamas. The Palestinians got what they elected, a government dedicated to the annihilation of Israel. If somebody wanted to annulated me, or my family and friends, I would want to kill them before they killed me and mine. The world condemning Israel for its actions views the Palestinians as rebels, or revolutionaries. Not all revolutions are for the good of the people. Look at some of the Coups we have seen. We have seen and participated in coups in Nicaragua, Chili, San Salvador, El Salvador, and were prepared to participate in a coup with rebels against Fidel Castro. Castro's friend and fellow revolutionary Chi Rivera's poster hangs in Obama campaign offices. Other world revolutionaries were people like Lenin and Stalin.

What would we do? What would any country do if attacked? It would retaliate. What if the world would have condemned

Bush for his "Shock and Awe" . . . Most thought it was brilliant. Some did condemn Bush but at that time Bush had a approval rating above 90% for his response. The highest of any president. Even higher than President-elect Obama. Isn't Israel's response the equivalent of Shock and Awe?

Now President-elect Obama wants to broker peace between Hamas, the Palestinians and Israel offering them a third option. He seems to think he is the messiah, the chosen one, the only one who can broker a peace between two nations that want to annihilate each other. War has been going on in some form or another, in the same region of the world since the beginning of time. Of course President-elect Obama hasn't spelled out his third option or how he can broker peace in this region. Just empty promises.

Biden said President Obama would be tested. And he will be. And President-elect Obama is being tested. With the current political atmosphere and the war, how could he not. All presidents are tested; it is their response that will encourage further testing. Bush's Shock and Awe response kept us safe for eight years. So far I have been disappointed in President-elect Obama's lack of condemnation for this Palestinian induced conflict. More than that, are some of the current situations a result of President-elect Obama's perceived lack of strength and experience based upon his own naive comments during the election? This is not a test of Bush it's a test of Obama.

One big difference between the Iraq war and previous wars is the effect on the economy. War usually creates jobs. Prosperity usually goes hand in hand with war but not this time.

President-elect Obama's choice to head the CIA, Leon Panetta is against any form of discomfort to the enemy. Anyone that has been a victim of domestic violence or a Prisoner of War would agree that water boarding is torture. Any clear thinking person would agree. Does water boarding compare with what the Viet Cong did in Viet Nam, sodomizing prisoners with a cattle prod? Skinning people alive? Does the degradation and humiliation at Abu Grebes or disrespecting the Koran at GITMO even compare with what our enemies have done to our troupes? Does it compare to 9/11? Is the moral high ground worth one American life? Will the Obama administration be the demise of the CIA? Will Americans be as safe under the Obama administration as it was under the Bush administrations, 41 and 43?

President-elect Obama told George Stephanopoulos that he will close GITMO but that closing it is a little more difficult than Americans think. He went on to talk about contaminated evidence against very bad people that is complicated by "The Anglo-American Justice System." Now he is saying that it might take four years to close GITMO.

If President-elect Obama's comment of an Anglo-American Justice System isn't racist I don't know what is. The term Anglo (white) implies a different set of standards, values and laws for the whites than is applied to everyone else? An attitude that has permeated the African American community and needs to be put straight. *Hay, Mr. Obama the term is American Justice System and has nothing to do with Anglo.* If you obey the law you usually won't be arrested. As a Native American I find the term *Anglo-American Justice System* offensive. President-elect Obama's politics appear red, not Native American red but socialist red. Are Obama's true colors coming out?

President-elect Obama tells George Stephanopoulos that under his administration everybody would have to sacrifice. This is a change from his election comments. He says "Everybody had to have some skin in the games." ***This is not a game this is our lives he is playing with.*** He never answers a question directly, hedging his beliefs. During the interview we are treated to the same indecision nobody noticed on the campaign trail. Each day my concerns for the future of our country grow.

> *"Don't change beliefs, transform the*
> *believer"*
> *-Werner Erhardt*
> *founder of est*

Obama says he will remove the troupes from Iraq in eighteen months, and Press Secretary Robert Gibbs says sixteen months. I have news for these politicians; George W Bush signed the Status of Forces Agreement with Iraq. Conditions of this agreement say America must remove troupes from urban areas by July 2009. The agreement calls for a complete withdrawal of U.S. troops from Iraq by the end of 2011. This was on the news but I guess the new administration wasn't briefed on that fact. If Obama can bring the troupes home, in victory in 2010, more power to him. Bring them home victorious, not with our tail between our legs the way we did in Viet Nam.

When I saw a report on uranium dipped weapons I contacted Senator Diane Feinstein. I was appalled when environmentalist Senator Feinstein wrote back saying she supports the use of uranium dipped weapons in Iraq. This at the same time supporting protection of the California Red Legged Frog. No double standard here. It's ok to contaminate the Iraqi environment, just not my (her) environment. Just don't build a hydroelectric plant in my neighborhood because it might impact the deer herd. I am all for protecting the environment but whose environment and at what cost?

Hello. Is anybody listening?

"Prudence, indeed, will dictate that governments long established, should not be changed for light and transient causes; and, accordingly, all experience [has] shown that mankind are more disposed to suffer while evils are sufferable than to right themselves

by abolishing the forms to which they are accustomed. But, when a long train of abuses and usurpations, pursuing invariably the same object, evinces a design to reduce [the people] under absolute despotism, it is their right, it is their duty, to throw off such government, and to provide new guards for their future security."

~Thomas Jefferson: Declaration of Independence, 1776

Guilt by Association

If a person actively seeks the company and friendships of members of the Klan, the Arian Brotherhood, the Skin Heads, the Crypts and the Bloods or any other radical group one could assume rightfully so that they supported the beliefs of these groups? In his own memoirs recorded in his own voice, Barrack Obama said "I covet my friendships very carefully", and when at Columbia, "I actively sought out friendships with known Marxist." Why is it so difficult for Obama supporters to believe Obama's own words? Is it that they don't know who Karl Marx is? For those of you who don't know, Karl Marx wrote a book named The Communist Manifesto which has become the bible of the communist movement. Does this make Obama a communist? That is something you will have to decide for yourself. I believe that he at least sympathizes with their views.

Candidate Obama has asked us to believe he sat in Jeremiah Wright's church, listening to him preach for twenty years and never heard anything like the sound bites we heard on Fox. Frankly I would have had more respect for Obama if he would have said he slept through Reverend Wright's inflammatory sermons. But they were too loud for anyone to sleep through. Was he paying attention, balancing his checkbook or perhaps working on his Blackberry? When I was fifteen I walked out of my church, never to return, after the minister made racially charged and political statements. I guess I had more integrity. But we know that for twenty years Obama sat in Reverend Wright his church, had Reverend Wright perform his marriage ceremony and even baptize his children. He prayed with him in the basement before Obama announced his candidacy. Jeremiah Write is said to have told Senator Obama that before the end of the election, he, Candidate Obama would have to disavow him (Wright). So how can we believe Obama didn't know any of these things? I remember early in the primaries, candidate Obama said that Wright was his "spiritual mentor" a man who had introduced him to Christianity. Jeremiah Wright was Senator and candidate Obama's minister, a man Obama a preacher whose words shocked the nation, words that Obama says he never heard. What was he doing sleeping through service? Or does he really agree with Reverend Wright? It took a while for candidate Obama to disavow Reverend Wright. After all, he said "I can no more disown [Wright] than I can disown my white grandmother," who "more than once has uttered racial or ethnic stereotypes that made me cringe," but when it became politically expedient he did just that. Not his grandmother but Reverend Wright. The newspapers report this but after the election Reverend Wright says when his daughter asks about the rift, he tells his own daughter there is no rift between the two of them. Later on after Wright's inflammatory remarks were exposed Obama said he wasn't his mentor.

If Wright introduced Obama to Christianity, what was Barry Obama before? Berry Obama was the name he used before he became Barack Obama. There are people who would have you believe Obama was Muslim. The facts are that when he was seven years old Barack Obama was registered in school as a Muslim by his white grandmother. Does that mean he was Muslim or merely a child whose parents were Muslim? He has said his mother was atheist. Candidate Obama has also said his parents instilled his values in him. Ok, his mother abandoned him to allow his grandmother to raise him. His grandmother did not change his religion. She was the one who registered him in school. So what values? He has also said his family was like a family straight out of central casting. Which movie, Deliverance?

Now we are being told that the anointed one came out of the muck and mire that has become Chicago politics as unscathed and pure as the driven snow. This would be like a Polar Bear climbing out of the La Brea Tar Pits coming out white and clean. It just doesn't happen.

The evidence leaked and released to the press shows Illinois Governor Blagojevich conspiring to sell President-elect Obama's barely used Senate Seat. Even most Democrats are up in arms about this and have told Blagojevich not to appoint a Senator and that they would not confirm whomever he appoints. Guess what? He does it anyway, appointing former Illinois attorney general Roland Burris, an African American. He probably is qualified, however when Democratic and African American Congressman Bobby Rush supports Blagojevich appointment of former Illinois attorney general Roland Burris because he would be the "only black in the Senate", it should be seen for what it is. Racist. Just because the racist is black doesn't mean it isn't racism. The reason Blagojevich selected a black man was because he wanted any disapproval of his appointment to appear as racist. I am sorry, being black is no reason to appoint or confirm. Neither is being white, Hispanic or any other nationality. I thought we needed the most qualified person for that position or any other political position. My dog is black but that doesn't make her qualified. And she's purebred. Furthermore Bobby Rush says Illinois shouldn't be deprived of having two Senators in the Senate. I surmise that Illinois hasn't had two Senators for the last two years, and based upon Senator Obama's voting record, they really haven't had two Senators in four years. What difference will a few more weeks make?

Roland Burris ran for Illinois governor, but the voters rejected him. He is told he won't be seated by Senate Majority Leader Harry Reed but he shows up to be seated anyway. He was not sworn in due to paperwork. Is he qualified? All reports say he is. But regardless of qualifications his nomination will always be tainted. Blagojevich should not have nominated anyone under the cloud of suspicion. Now reports surface that say Burris contributed

$15,000 to Blagojevich's campaign. Burris admits to helping Blagojevich get elected but says he never sat down and talked to him. Interesting . . . There is also the issue of how Burris's wife got her job. Harry Reed capitulated and Roland Burris was sworn in as the junior Senator from Illinois on January 15th, 2008.

Obama has tried to distance himself from Illinois Governor Blagojevich who tried to sell the senate seat but there is one problem. Senator Obama endorsed Blagojevich publicly on his campaign for governor. President-elect Obama was questioned by the F.B.I. for over two hours regarding his relationship with Blagojevich. Does that mean Obama did something wrong? No. It just means Barack Obama knows Blagojevich a little better than he admits.

As far as Blagojevich's guilt or innocence, that will play out in court. What was released by US Attorney Pat Fitzgerald indicated at the very least there was a conspiracy to sell the Senate seat.

President-elect Obama's selection of 70 year old Leon Panetta as C.I.A. Director even has Democrats including Diane Feinstein upset. Chairman of the Senate Intelligence Committee, Senator Feinstein questions

Leon Panetta's Intelligence experience. She should be questioning President-elect Obama's judgment in this as well as other appointments. The most likely choice for the position would have been President-elect Obama's Transition Team Intelligence Advisor Brennan, but he suddenly withdrew his name in November.

Bill Richardson, President-elect Obama's nominee for Commerce Secretary withdraws under Federal investigation in a Pay to Play scandal allegedly for exchanging government contracts for contributions to three of Richardson's political committees. It seems that former presidential candidate Bill Richardson is accused of awarding a $1.5 million dollar contract to a firm CDR that was not qualified. It has further been alleged that money from CDR was paid to two of Governor Bill Richardson's political action committees. Including money paid for Richardson and his family's transportation to the 2004 Boston Democratic National Convention. No quid pro quo here. How stupid do they think the American public is? Of course this was known in August and could have easily been discovered by President-elect Obama's Transition Team. Good vetting.

Candidate Obama promise change. It looks like that means bringing in the former presidential staff to run the country while like George W Bush, President-elect Obama dreams of being America's first king. Rather than place individuals in positions of experience, President-elect Obama seems to be shuffling the deck and it appears the Obama Cabinet is like a house of cards and any strong wind will blow it down.

It shouldn't surprise anyone when candidate Obama supported talks with our enemies. His lack of judgment and Naiveté and lack of understanding of worldwide political views allowed him to associate with terrorists like Bill Ayers. Barack Obama served on the Wood's foundation with Bill Ayers. They received a grant to Radicalize Education. We see what has come out of that radicalization. Our history books are rewritten to reflect the Liberalism and Socialist viewpoint. Frankly we have enough radicals. I don't want tax sponsored schools to radicalize students. When I think of radicals I think of organizations like the Black Panthers, the Weather Underground and the KKK. An armed Black Panther was videotaped during the election standing guard in front of a polling place. Voter intimidation was alleged. I would have been intimidated but I would have voted anyway. Nobody has the right to intimidate that right away. Radicalism and violence go hand in hand. It shouldn't surprise anyone when Obama wants to talk to Hamas or that he appointed Eric Holder who was influential in the pardons of Marc Rich and sixteen members of FALN.

The FALN a Puerto Rican terrorists group was only responsible for 120 bomb attacks on US targets. Of course you could go back and say these incidents occurred when Obama was just a child. So should Obama's judgment be called on for what someone did when he was eight years old? There is currently an eight year old in Phoenix, Arizona accused of premeditated murder. So who's to say what judgment an eight year old has but a forty year old should have better judgment. It is one thing to sit on a board with a person who made a mistake that they acknowledge but Bill Ayers doesn't think he did anything wrong. His wife Bernadette Dohrn did get convicted but the prosecution bungled the case against Ayers and couldn't even get a conviction with a confession. Bill Ayers responded "Guilty as hell. Free as a bird. God bless America"

The pictures are there for anyone who cares to look. Barry Obama has had friendships like that with Franklin Marshall Davis, an avowed communist that Barry Obama in his memoirs refers to as his mentor. He has had membership in Committees like the Democratic Socialists of America, a party that Senator Obama was a member of through a spin off called the New Party.

Formed in 1992 the Committees for Correspondence for Democracy and Socialism (CCDS) is, after Democratic Socialists of America (DSA) and Communist Party USA (CPUSA), the third largest most influential Marxist group in the USA, all groups are influential in Chicago politics, New York and California politics along with some other centers in the union movement and in black communities. These organizations backed candidate Obama for president. Does the fact that these people backed Obama mean that his views reflect their views? They believe it does.

Now Carol Browner is expected to be named energy czar, the chief of energy and environmental issues under Obama. Carol Browner served until the summer of 2008 as a member of a socialist organization, Socialist

International, the umbrella group for 170 "social democratic, socialist and labor parties" in 55 countries, whose mission is to enact progressive government policies, including toward environmental concerns like climate change. Here goes the environmental climate change movement again. Less than a week ago the Russian scientists said we are going into an ice age.[4]

I find with each click of the mouse the web of deceit lies and dubious association grows. What of Obama's association with ACORN (the Association of Community Organizations for Reform Now)? Both before and during the election.

When Obama was elected President the congratulations came in. Worldwide. From Syrian President Bashar al-Assad, Hugo Chavez of Venezuela, Fidel Castro of Cuba, Iranian President Mahmoud Ahmadinejad, Russian President Dmitry Medvedev, Argentina's President Cristina Kirchner. The list goes on. Now I understand sending congratulations but these people supported Obama's election. Some of these people may have even contributed to Obama's campaign through untraceable transactions but the

---

[4] http://en.rian.ru/science/20080122/97519953.html

public will never know. Are my enemy's friends not also my enemies?

We also have Senator Obama's affiliation with real estate investor and slumlord Tony Rezko.

While most Americans are struggling just to pay their mortgage the Obama's land the deal of the century. Mrs. Rezko, with an income of $37,500 a year and assets of $35,000 purchased the vacant property at 5050 South Greenwood Avenue with a down payment of $125,000 and $500,000 mortgage for the original asking price of $625,000. Now it's hard enough to find financing on vacant property even with sufficient income. But the numbers don't make sense. Furthermore the property the Rezkos bought they sold a ten foot strip of property to the Obamas. This made the Rezko property substandard and therefore undevelopable. So in essence they gave the Obama's a piece of property they bought at $625,000 for chump change. No quid pro quo here.

British-Iraqi billionaire Nadhmi Auchi, one of Britain's wealthiest men, helped Mr. Obama to buy the Georgian mansion in Chicago where he lives. Mr. Auchi, who has been conviction for corruption in France, registered the loan to Antoin "Tony" Rezko, on May 23, 2005. Three weeks later the Obamas bought the house on the South Side of the city, while Mrs. Rezko bought the garden plot next door. It might also be noted it was from the same seller on the same day, June 15. This should be investigated further.

I don't believe in guilt by association I believe in guilt by actions. These people call Obama's judgment into question. Nothing more.

Ingrid Mattson has been asked to speak at the inauguration prayer service. She is a Muslim scholar and leader of the Islamic Society of North America with ties to the Holy Land Foundation. This group has contributed to the terrorist group Hamas. Linda Davis of the Obama camp says she (Ingrid Mattson) has a "stellar reputation in the faith community."

With all the corruption in Washington and the Obama administration's selections, Nancy Pelosi with help from the head of the Judiciary Committee, John Conyers wants to prosecute members of the Bush administration. For what, keeping us safe for the last seven years?

The way I picture President Obama's first day in the White House is standing there with wife Michelle, naked, throwing billions of dollars in the air.

Obama's and the voters Naiveté is frightening!

"We cannot expect the Americans to jump from capitalism to Communism, but we can assist their elected leaders in giving Americans small doses of socialism until they suddenly awake to find they have Communism."

~ Soviet Leader Nikita Khrushchev, 1959

Medicare and Healthcare

Under President-elect Obama's proposed healthcare plan you would be forced into buying insurance. This is not free. You have to pay for it. The Democrats seem more concerned with health insurance than they are with healthcare. I have health insurance, what I don't have is healthcare. It is very difficult to find a doctor that will accept a new insurance or Medicare patient. With what Medicare pays doctors I can't blame them. I am embarrassed to ask a doctor to accept Medicare.

The media and President-elect Obama tells you Medicare is bankrupt but as a Medicare recipient I can tell you that we received a letter saying that due to a surplus in the Medicare fund there would be no increase in our monthly 2009 Medicare cost. So which is it? Surplus or bankrupt? Somebody is lying.

The government wants to control what you put into your body, not only in the way of drugs but also food. We already have a consumption tax on alcohol and cigarettes and now states like New York want to add a consumption tax on sugar soda and candy. And Congress wants to add 61¢ tax on a pack of cigarettes. This is to pay for their added child healthcare costs. What happens when people quit smoking? They are going to have to find another special interest group to pay for their programs. The tax on sugar products equates to nothing more than an obesity tax. The reasoning for this tax is that obese people have a higher healthcare costs than non-obese people.

The Government has put a ban on triglycerides and Trans Fats used in fast food restaurants and then in sit-down restaurants. Wendy's French fries taste like they are fried in motor oil. Soon you will not be able to buy the products of your choice at your local grocer.

Congress wastes money on Athlete Steroids and HGH use. Athletes are charged with lying to Congress even if they didn't lie. Because Congress *believes* they must have used HGH. This is about like assuming there are California Red Legged Frogs because you couldn't find them and diminishes the presumption of innocence.

We begin by putting our children on vitamins that recent reports shows do no good in preventing disease, then on to Ritalin because they are acting up, then Paxil because they are depressed so we can brainwash them. I have often wondered how drugs effected the election. The FDA refuses to put a black box warning on Ritalin, a form of amphetamine yet they put one on asthma medicine that doesn't contain steroids. If you listen to the advertisements people are more likely to die if using the ones that contain the steroids.

Personally, I believe that what a person puts in their body or takes out of their body is their own business, not the governments or the church.

It seems to me that Liberal FOX newscaster Alan Colmes is the poster child of the Kool-Aid drinkers that were so easily controlled by the media. Blank stares, like deer caught in the headlights were the most obvious sign of the Obama voter. He mindlessly chants 95% tax rebates but has no idea of his surroundings.

According to Ann Coulter taxpayers spend $112 billion on unwed mothers. I remember a news interview of a welfare mother who said the taxpayers should pay her to stay home and take care of her children. She stated that she believed the only way to raise upstanding citizens was for their mothers to stay home and take care of their children. In order to insure she and her children had a future, the welfare department was paying her tuition to Stanford. With your tax dollars. Having a child should be a matter of choice, not accident, not to increase welfare or child support payments, or to make you feel like a woman or a man. Every child deserves to be wanted. And no woman should be forced to bear a child she does not want. It is not fair to the child.

Adoption rights have changed from when women had the ultimate say to men's rights which have resulted in adopted children being removed from loving homes because an unemployed teenaged father wants custody. Birth records which were once sealed are now open to adopted children.

The courts refuse to make a bastard of a child when a married man challenges, rightfully so the genetics of his child. In other words, if you bought it, you own it. As long as a father supports a child, regardless if it is his biological child he is on the hook. Miss a child support payment and you risk losing your driver's license, hunting and fishing license etc. When you lose your driver's license you can't work, especially if you are a truck driver. Frankly, I don't believe in child support. In this day and age when a woman has a choice, and the ability to earn a living at the same rate as her male counterpart, and she wants custody, then the mother should be responsible for supporting that child. I have seen too many men, barely able to survive while the ex-wife takes Caribbean vacations and puts powder up her nose. On the money the man has paid to support his children. It's not fair, and it's not morally right.

As a smoker, I am now going to be forced to subsidize the Obama Children's Health Insurance Program. I didn't give birth to your child, why should I be forced to support your child? This healthcare program is said to mimic the program which they just cancelled in Hawaii. The reason they cancelled the Hawaii program is because people discovered if they cancelled their insurance the taxpayers would foot the bill. In short, it didn't work.

Nancy Pelosi says Obama will shake up and settle entitlement (Social Security) reform. When asked about a reduction of benefits she states "nothing is off the table." Including cutting your Social Security and Medicare benefits.

"From each according to his ability to each according to his needs"
-Karl Marx

The Media R.I.P.

We have already seen the demise of
freedom of the press, freedom of speech
and freedom of privacy. Just ask Joe the
Plumber. The government already has the
power to tap our phones and monitor our
emails. What else will they have under the
Obama, Pelosi and Reid trifecta? A repeal of
the drilling initiative they just passed? A
demise of our National Security? Candidate
Obama couldn't even pass a basic DOD
Security Clearance and now President
Obama will have accessed to our most
sensitive information. He says he wants to
cut defense spending but increase the
military. How is he going to do that without
instituting a draft? Nikita Khrushchev's said
he would bury us from within. Is his
prophesy coming to fruition? Is President
Obama's form of Socialism/Marxism and
Communism the future of democracy?

Instead of discussing the issues the
American news media concentrates on which
breed Obama's dog should be if (when) he
gets elected. If his children wanted a dog
they should have gotten one regardless of the
outcome of the election. A dog is a
commitment for life, not an accessory to

show the public that they the Obamas are just like us.

The media focused on the supposedly $150,000 the Republican National Committee spent on Sarah Palin and her families clothes and makeup during the election. Frankly, that's a bargain. She was and should have been seen as a Republican product which has to be marketed. If she were to have kept the clothes she is required to declare it on her income tax. This was no different than renting any wardrobe. Compare candidate Palin's wardrobe to Hillary's "traveling (polyester) pant suits." And the fashion challenged men who were color coordinating her wardrobes with the backdrops. They could have taken lesions from Nancy Pelosi's "girlfriends." Even looking like a drag queen is better than looking like the polyester queen.

On the other hand, candidate Obama paid $820,000 to ACORN for "stage lighting"; oh excuse me, to get out the vote. That's a few hundred thousand more than Sarah Palin's wardrobe. Then the left wing complains that Sarah Palin revised her travel reports regarding her children's travel. For the bull Governor Palin has put up with for the American people Governor Palin is a true

Patriot. The crucifixion of Governor Palin is a sad point in our nation's history and exactly the reason I decided not to go into politics. One vice presidential candidate had a history of mental illness and he was forced to withdraw. So many years ago. I think his name was Eagleton, forgotten in the myriad of failed politicians.

Governor Palin's daughter was criticized. Compare the treatment of Governor Palin and her family, a family that did not ask to be in the spotlight to the Obama family. Obama said his wife and children were off limits. The media respected the Obama family but not the Palin family. Just another way the media and the information dissemination to the public were controlled.

The Democrats want Equal access to AM radio stations and that would be great if it worked both ways. How about equal time on television for John McCain after Obama's infomercial? That would have been a good start. The Democrats only care about AM radio because of Conservative talk show hosts like Sean Hannity and rush Limbaugh and they want to reinstitute the Fairness Doctrine. This could put Conservative talk radio out of business because if you can't get sponsorship and ratings for Liberal talk radio you would be forced to cancel the Conservative radio show. Silencing the Conservative opposition is just what they want. If you disagree with the Liberal viewpoint you will be silenced. Just like Ann Coulter when she was (temporarily) banned from the Today show because the producer didn't like the comments about Obama in her newest book. They did rebook her, but only after the bad publicity.

During the election I talked to people to try to understand why people would vote for their candidate. One of the people I talked to was my husband's dentist at the SFVAMC. He didn't believe Obama (or McCain) would escalate the war in Afghanistan. We just did. 30,000 more troupes were called up to go to Afghanistan. The most disturbing statement my husband's dentist made was he said we could use more socialism and less democracy. I could have fallen over and I really don't want my husband to use this man as his dentist anymore. It's sad but this is how I feel about anyone who voted for Obama. I don't hang with Communists. I do covet my friendships carefully.

Another person I talked to didn't even know who Karl Marx was, or what Marxism or Socialism is all about. This was a Hispanic friend. He wanted to know why I abandoned my support for Senator Clinton and rather than support Obama, a Democrat, instead chose to support Senator McCain. When I explained it to him about Marxism he said he would tell his wife and friends to vote McCain. He just didn't know. Another person told me he was voting for Obama "to shake things up." Obama will shake things up. But not in the way most people want. You bought it, now somebody's going to have to pay the bills. With a 7.2% unemployment rate that is predicted to go to double digits.

Obama has consistently said this (wife, children, and religion) or that (Ayers or ACORN) is off limits, and everything negative is called on is a distraction. Yet Obama's surrogates and the media have been ruthless against Sarah Palin. I offer that this. The only thing the Democrats have against Governor Palin is she is not Senator Clinton. They know it will probably be Palin in 2012, and that scares the hell out of them. They have no choice but to attack and try to discredit Governor Palin.

Like a dog begging for a steak the media drooled all over Obama while misrepresenting him to the American public.

He Kicked reporters off his plane after an unflattering report appeared in their newspaper. President-elect Obama controlled the media with all the skill of a master puppeteer.

While I was writing this book and checking my facts I came across Internet monitored sites which stated that if you clicked on this link your activities would be monitored. What happened to freedom of speech? What happened to an open exchange of ideas and intelligent thinking in the Obama Nation? All the while the world explodes in violence.

Rather than blaming Hamas for the violence in Gaza the Palestinians blame America. Violent protests erupt on the steps of the US Embassy in Beirut Lebanon after a one week cease fire took place between Hamas and Israel.

All the while Obama criticizes Bush and depresses American's expectations. He takes on the easy issues while leaving the hard decisions regarding the war to Bush. Then condemns Bush for any action taken. What happens when Obama wakes up in the White House actually has to make a decision? As PBS Washington Week Moderator Gwen

Ifell put it he could "get in there and **_actually have to do something_** about Gaza."

Voter Ignorance and Gay Marriage

As the presumptive Democratic nominee you have to ask yourself why Senator Clinton lost. As a HillStar volunteer I can give my perspective on her campaign.

I wasn't surprised when the caller ID on my phone showed the name Hillary Clinton, after all I was busy developing political support for my grant proposal so when the caller ID showed Hillary Clinton, I answered the phone "Hello, Senator Clinton." The voice on the other end of the line asked "How did you know?" My response was simply "Caller ID." Now I don't know if it really was Senator Clinton, it did sound like her, or maybe it was just a surrogate that simply went along with my assumption. She asked if I would volunteer to work on her HillStar campaign. I said I would be honored she gave me the time and address and asked if I needed directions. I said I would get them off the internet. Nothing more. Just a brief conversation. I drove the 215 miles to her San Francisco headquarters.

A small flight of stairs led to the doorway and two flights of narrow subsiding stairs led up to the headquarters. Like children we

were told to put our names on cut out blue
construction paper stars to be posted on the
wall. We were treated to stale bagels and an
inaudible training session. We were told to
have coffees where we invite our friends to
make political cold calls. We walked out
empty handed and confused. Disappointed I
found that Hillary Clinton's supporters
couldn't even motivate people who wanted to
be motivated. I came out with the sense of
how little I knew about Senator Clinton's
policies and with the knowledge that she
probably would lose the election.

Along comes Barrack Hussein Obama,
Tabula Rasa the blank slate. With no history
he became all things to all people. To the
antiwar movement he became the
embodiment of peace. They didn't listen
when he said he would escalate the war in
Afghanistan, only that he voted against the
war in Iraq. As a state Senator when his vote
didn't count. The Obama voters didn't hear
his commitment to disarm the Strategic Air
Defense, or reduce defense spending while at
the same time increasing enlistment. Senator
Clinton told us what little experience Obama
had and how he voted present more often
than he voted pro or con. A mugwamp, a
fence sitter. Someone who can't make a

decision. We believed Senator Clinton. Then she turned on us to support the anointed one. She stares at Obama with the starry eyed stare of a sixteen year old with her first crush. She abandoned her supporters.

Obama served as Illinois Senator for less than 18months before he began his candidacy for president. Barack Obama must have cojones that drag the ground.

Candidate Obama said he supported gay rights but Candidate and then President-elect Obama said he was against gay marriage. So he got the gay vote. Now supporters of California's Prop 8 including Congressman Barney Frank have realized that their messiah doesn't agree with gay marriage. Even though he told them he didn't during the election. Is the honeymoon over? California voters voted to define marriage as a union between a man and a woman. Gays didn't like it and protested at the churches especially those of Church of Latter Day Saints. The LDS Church, better known as Mormons came out actively against the gay marriage amendment but so did the Catholic Church. Now they start protesting and defacing Catholic churches. But only a couple of Catholic churches. Reports show up to 84% of Catholics voted yes on Prop 8.

70% of the black vote went for Prop 8. So why isn't the gay movement protesting black churches and more Catholic churches? Simple, because it would be labeled as racist. Especially if they protested the black churches. Now blacks are rioting in Oakland because a transit officer executed an unarmed man. I don't understand how a person can think if they riot and destroy their own belongings, their own hometown that it furthers their cause. I have supported gay and race relations but when gays and blacks riot I lose sympathy.

Joe Biden says if it walks like a duck and quacks like a duck it must be a duck. Well if it looks like a socialist and talks like a socialist, it must be a socialist.

Barney Frank is up in arms because President-elect Obama invited Jeff Warren to his multimillion dollar inauguration. Would he prefer Jeremiah Wright?

This is the most lavished and expensive inauguration (coronation) in history, during a time of financial crisis. With a Cadillac Mentality reminiscent of Kim Jung Il's lavish extravaganza (while the starving North Korean masses didn't have electricity or food) the carbon footprint of the Obama coronation is projected by the Institute for

Liberty to exceed 575 million pounds of CO2. They go on to say that it would take the average household, like you and me, a mere 57,598 years to generate a similar carbon footprint.[5] Who's paying for this? The Obama people say they are. Even if the ceremony is paid for by donors there is still the extensive amount of behind the scenes cost like cleanup and security that is eventually born by tax dollars. Millions of people are expected to attend this lavish party. Expected to cost over $170 million dollars taxpayers are paying more than half the cost. Obama raised $45 million dollars for the inauguration. Tax payers will pay $125 million more or less. Taxpayers are paying for the police and secret service, city employees, maintenance workers, porta-pottys etc? I guess this is another of Obama's idea of spreading the wealth around. To give the most lavished party in history. The Obama campaign describes the inauguration as a "Celebration of Common Values." Decadent consumptive excess is not my values. Isn't this too flashy, too decadent for the most somber office in the nation?

---

[5] http://thechillingeffect.org/2009/01/14/ifl-inauguration-will-produce-575-million-pounds-of-co2/

Republican Tom Dashiell calls for canceling this celebration due to the economic times. Wouldn't a quiet televised inauguration be more dignified, more appropriate for the highest office, in this financially critical time? Wouldn't it be better to spend most of that money helping the communities that Obama says are in dire need? Donated the money to the Red Cross for food for the homeless instead of building Greek Columns? I wonder with temperatures in the low 30s, how many people will become ill due to their attendance in the freezing cold? How many people will die from exposure to the cold? Wouldn't it be ironic? The weatherman predicts rain, possible snow.

The Obama crowds are reminiscent of another leader some seventy years ago. Isn't politics about serving the people and not self service? I am really bothered by the cheering crowds, one arm reaching to the sky. If you ask most of Obama's adorning worshipers few would even know who the Speaker of the House is.

Congress has a 10% voter approval. The worst in history and even worse than President George W, (would be King) Bush. With such a low Congressional approval, why would voters reelect the same people?

Not only did they reelect Nancy Pelosi who was then reelected Speaker of the House for the 111ᵗʰ Session of Congress, and Harry Reid, they topped the trifecta with Barrack Hussein (I want to bankrupt any electric generating facility that uses coal) Obama.

The only answer can be voter ignorance. Few voters seem to know the issues and will base their vote on one single issue. I met a man at the San Francisco Medical Center. We got to talking because of my dog. He said he voted for Nancy Pelosi because he had an eight year old child and she spoke against gay marriage. I ask him if he knew why she wouldn't allow an up or down vote on offshore drilling and he said he didn't. Most people vote because of belief, appearance or party affiliation and most don't even know what their party stands for.

Up until now the Democrat has been the blue collar worker and the Republicans were considered the white collar, educated voter. The Democrats were the Union workers; they represented the hardworking everyday American. The Republicans ran the businesses, Wall Street, etc. When did the brands change? During the 2008 election the Democrat voter was described as collage educated. Implying the Republicans weren't.

This myth was put forth by the text messaging i-m-generation. Most of them can text message and play video games but they have never read the Constitution. And most will end up with Carpel Tunnel and tendinitis becoming crippled by their electronic addictions. Obama will leave the White House four years behind on Blackberry technology or maybe not. He has told the Secret Service he intends to keep his Blackberry. Will the information be available to the public? Probably not.

I became skeptical of the American voter several years ago. At the time I worked with a lady named Thelma Black. Thelma stated she was going to vote for Jimmy Carter because "Ford had to be punished for pardoning Nixon." I saw it differently. The country was mired in the muck of Watergate, much in the same way the country became absorbed in the Monica Lewinski scandal when Bill Clinton stated that "I did not have sex with that woman." So anyway, the country was so obsessed with whether or not Richard Nixon would be impeached and tried. In order to stimulate the economy and get the country going again, Gerald Ford pardoned Nixon. So that was how a peanut farmer got elected to the White House.

Jimmy Carter has been labeled as the worst president in history. Unable to keep military secrets he, President Jimmy Carter announced to the public that Northrop Corporation was building the super secret stealth bomber. Employees couldn't admit or deny what the President said. During his presidency Jimmy Carter cancelled production of nuclear submarines and the B-1 bomber program, putting the aerospace and defense industry in an economic tailspin, jeopardizing our National Security and setting back future defense projects. Kind of sounds like Obama.

During the 2008 campaign Obama said he was about change, but when pressed neither he nor his surrogates or proponents couldn't answer what type of change. When cornered, like a cornered dog, the surrogates and Obama would go on the attack and labeling McCain was Bush Three. I suspected Senator Obama had a chance so I wanted to find out what his politics were. You couldn't. Not on mainstream media. So I started researching.

Candidate Obama told us about his family. A grandmother who's perceived racist comments often made him cringe. A grandmother who was obviously suffering from PTSD from a previous encounter with a black man. He told us they would say he wasn't like the other presidents on the dollar bill. And oh by the way he told us he was "black." I didn't know that. I thought he was African American. He played the race card while blaming the Republicans. Bigotry is still bigotry and reverse bigotry, voting for a man because of his color is just as discriminatory as voting against a man for his color.

Governor and Vice presidential candidate Sarah Palin was harassed and crucified because she was a woman. That didn't seem to bother Obama as he referred to a news reporter dismissively as "Sweetie." Sexism doesn't seem to carry the stigma as racism.

During the election there was an effigy of Governor Palin hung by a noose as a Halloween decoration. The police said it was acceptable because Governor Palin was a white woman, however, if it would have been Barrack Obama or a black woman it would have been considered a hate crime because it would have been considered racially motivated. No double standard here. There are crimes of greed and crimes of passion but it seems to me crimes of violence are all hate crimes and one word should not change the classification. Who knew it was ok to hang a woman? But not a person of color . . . Somehow that was exactly what the media did to Sarah Palin. They convicted her and hung her without a trial.

The Internet information age allowed candidate Obama to raise an unprecedented amount of untraceable campaign contributions from dead people, foreigners and even dead fish. Interestingly he selected Rahm Emanuel as Chief of Staff. Rahm Emanuel once sent a dead fish to a reporter he disagreed with. A somewhat humorous attempt at intimidation. But the internet gave us unlimited information. Overwhelming information twenty-four hours a day. Sound bites went viral and once on the internet nothing could stop the flow of information, disinformation, news and blogs. It became clear as tar. Hours are spent researching to find a glimmer of truth.

Sound bites became daily fodder. Sound bites give you a glimpse into the motives of a person but sound bites can be and are manipulated. So you have to listen carefully. Does the sound bite show a pattern as in Jeremiah Wright's speeches or are they manipulated for political gain as when the

Obama campaign clipped John McCain's comments about the economy. John McCain said "the fundamentals of economy are strong but we have some real problems." Do you see something missing from the sound bite?

How did Republicans loose the under 30 vote 2 to 1? Lack of education. When interviewed the Obama supporter didn't know the Democrats were in charge of Congress during the last two years of the Bush Administration. Giving the vote to the 18 year old voter was a mistake. Americans who supported this felt that if an eighteen year old could go to war then they should be allowed to vote. I have a different proposal. Increase the enlistment age. The average eighteen year old has very little understanding of politics and are easily influenced by a dynamic speaker and a celebrity endorsement. Eighteen year olds are quite simply too easily brainwashed.

I don't want actors telling me who to vote for. They spend their whole life pretending to be something or someone other than who they are. They are actors. They are singers. Who out there thinks Britney Spears is stable enough to recommend a good drycleaner much less a good politician? How about taking political advice from Keith Richards? Or Paris Hilton? Wait a minute, Obama supporters did take political advice from Paris Hilton. How many actors and musicians destroy their own lives through drugs and alcohol? Yet they think we should listen to them? And our politicians, at least the Democratic candidates want us to take our political advice from them. The eighteen year old does listen. Another problem with the eighteen year old vote and even military induction is they are easily manipulated. Perhaps we should change the minimum voting and induction age to thirty-five?

How do we trust the elections? How do we trust the media? Mainstream media says Al Franken won the Minnesota election after the most fraudulent recount in history. Norm Coleman won but the recount changed that. The Wall Street Journal reports 25% of Minnesota precincts had more ballots than voters who signed in to vote. And twenty-five precincts had more votes than voters. Ballots were found in the trunks of cars and churches were searched for missing ballots. This one will and should end up in court. Harry Reed says he will not allow Norm Coleman back in the Senate. The Democratic Secretary of State Katherine

Harris says there is no voter fraud here. Its transparent. Apparently transparency means clear as mud in Minnesota. The Republicans have threaten to filibuster if Al Franken tries to be seated.

The issue of voter registration fraud verses voter fraud was a major issue in this campaign when ACORN registered dead fish, dead people and people multiple times. When anybody can go to the US Post Office and obtain a voter registration form, why do we need to pay groups like ACORN to strong arm register voters? This is another waste of tax dollars.

One positive thing that resulted from Obama winning the election is as a friend told me Blacks can no longer play racial victim and blame whites for holding them back. After all, anybody can grow up to be president, even if his birth records are questionable. Any man that is. In many ways the election of Obama hurt race relations. Too many people think Obama was elected because of race and if he fails it will only be fodder for those who don't think a black man can do the job. I think qualifications are more important than race or gender. I just haven't been able to find them here. Racial profiling is racial profiling regardless whose side you are on.

Millions of people will be at the Obama inauguration. Personally, I would like to see a caravan of dump trucks full of acorns form a convoy and dump them at the inauguration.

So who were the Obama voters? One recent news broadcast showed one of the Obama voters. This man was in his twenties, voting for the first time and was autistic. One man I know who supported and voted for Obama is a quadriplegic with severe brain injury sustained in a car accident. After the accident he had the mentality of about a six year old. He voted for Obama because he is gay. Seventy-five percent of the Hispanic voter voted for Obama. And thanks to ACORN they got out the homeless vote and the skid row vote. And we can't forget the felon vote. I always thought convicted felons were stripped of their right to vote. There was also the Democrat who votes Democrat no matter what and has no idea of their party's stance on any of the issues. And of course you have the wife who votes the same way her husband does. When I first registered to vote in 1970 my then husband, an abusive tyrant, told me I would register

and vote Republican. I registered
Independent. This is the one area where
nobody should be able to pressure you.
Think for yourself. If you don't nobody else
will.

The biggest contributing factor to the
Obama election was voter ignorance. The
typical voter gets his or her news from
mainstream media. Ten minutes of politics
while cooking dinner, helping the kids with
their homework, relaxing having a beer or
doing a plethora of things while trying to be
somewhat informed. I know. I was one of
those people. Until I made an intentional
choice to educate myself. The questions I
had were not being answered by the
mainstream media. I started watching CNN
and FOX in addition to MSNBC and CBS. I
started watching Washington Today and the
Senate Hearings and the House of
Representatives. I watch about six hours per
day to be informed and even at that the bull
and methane comes flying at the rotary
oscillator with such velocity that I can't keep
up.

The man I met In San Francisco who said
he voted for Nancy Pelosi said he did so
because she spoke at an anti Proposition 8
rally and he didn't want his eight year old

daughter to be exposed to gay marriage issues. I wonder if Nancy Pelosi's gay constituency knew about her anti gay marriage stance.

Obama holds daily press conferences to indoctrinate Americans to his view. He holds a luncheon with the Conservative press and a separate one with the Liberal press. EJ Dionne from the Brookings Institute describes it to Stephanopoulos saying that it was like "Professor Obama teaching a seminar on how you deal with a whole lot of crisis at the same time and stay calm." He wants a "New Declaration of Independence." Is Obama taking his words from Will Smith or is this the first sign of a desire to overthrow the Constitution?

So what happened to the Republican Brand? Where did the Contract with America go? We need to demand a Code of Conduct from our legislatures and the media and hold them to a higher standard than the average American. We must question satire used not for humor but to defame.

Where do we go from here? I say hold on for the bumpiest ride of your life. The economy is in a freefall. The world is in turmoil and the Americans have elected change and inexperience. I hope President

Obama succeeds beyond his wildest dreams not as a socialist but as a Capitalist, an American, in a Democratic Society for the people and by the people. We also have to have the courage to ask if Obama fails then what?

I hope if Obama does fail he has the courage to do the right thing.

Trust Me

When I was growing up anytime someone said "trust me", it seemed they were trying to get into my pants. Yet that is what President-elect Obama is saying. Trust me to create more jobs, more government and more debt. Marketing the message that the economy is going to get worse before it gets better he is already running for a second term. If things get worse he will tell you I told you so and blame Bush, if by some miracle the economy improves Obama will take all the credit and present himself as a hero. If you watch the stock market you will see as Obama speaks stocks go down. He blames corporate America, Wall Street and Bush's policies for all economic woes yet it was the Democrats who proposed more regulation and it was that very regulation, sponsored by a Democrat ran Congress whose policies allowed the mortgage meltdown.

Now Nancy Pelosi wants to bar Republicans from introducing alternative bills to Democrat sponsored bills. Get a clue Nancy, not everybody voted Democrat. We want our voice heard too. Nobody elected you Queen.

Pornographer Larry Flint is asking Congress for aid to the pornography industry with bailout money. Yea you read that right. I guess even in these economic times the pornography industry is suffering. Personally I think that's a good thing.

Even the casinos in Los Vegas have their hands out because gaming is down. Then the mayor wants you to build a museum dedicated to the Mob with your tax dollars. Do Floridians really need more waterslides or a Polar Bear exhibit? Isn't that taking an endangered species and against the EPA and Endangered Species Act? I guess the rules don't apply when it's for exhibiting a species but not for development or the benefit of mankind.

President-elect Obama tells Americans we must be prepared to sacrifice yet recently, when the lights went out when he was on vacation in Hawaii, the Governor sent a generator to the Obama vacation home to make sure his family didn't suffer. I have suffered for nine years without grid connected electricity. I have lost my five year old dog to the heat because I couldn't run an air conditioner. Don't tell me about suffering and giving things up. Or having some skin in the game. I haven't had a vacation in more than eight years. I have been tethered to my electric system, unable to leave my house for more than one day. I bought into their green, renewable energy lies. It has cost me everything. Congress functions with a lead bunker isolationist mentality asking that the masses sacrifice while Congress and the Obamas live in the lap of luxury, spreading your wealth around to their friends and cronies. *A Government of the* People, *by the* People *and for the* People. That is what our Constitution says. They work for us. Not the other way around but Congress has forgotten to read the Constitution.

The rules don't apply equally to the government officials, Congress and even presidents alike believe they are above the law. The disabled veteran who uses a Service Dog can be denied access to any church or government building. My husband was denied access to the Chico VA Medical Center. The government exempts its self from the very laws that it legislates for everyone else and is sworn to protect.

Now President-elect Obama wants to spend Trillion in infrastructure. *A stimulus package that does not include a National Highway Program.* How soon will this infrastructure get built? Five years? Ten years? Never? Billions will be spent, on environmental impact studies and processes but the likelihood of rebuilding our infrastructure during the Obama Administration is slim. Green jobs riding bicycles will be created. Perhaps we will create jobs with rickshaw taxis in New York. We will have to get rid of the horse drawn carriages, they produce too much methane. The money will be spent. The nation will be bankrupt and we will be deep in the Obama Depression. Ask yourself, not if you are better off now than you were eight years ago, but rather if you are better off now than you were on November 3rd, 2008.

What if you wanted to control an election and bring down the world economy? All you would have to do is buy up stocks in oil and CNG, control the prices through speculation and at just the right time have the Treasury Secretary announce the economy is on the verge of collapse unless the government converted immediately to Socialism.

"The advance of liberalism...
[encourages] the hope that the human mind

will some day get back to the freedom it enjoyed two thousand years ago."

~Thomas Jefferson to John Adams, 1821

Death of a Nation

On November 4, 2008 at 8:01 PM Pacific Standard Time, Democracy died. I say this because the election was called before one single West Coast vote was counted. The Electoral College was at 203 to 147 when the race was called. In one state, I believe it was Colorado, John McCain had 75% of the vote, and in New Mexico he had 66% of the vote but the news networks including FOX called those states and the election for Obama. No matter whom you voted for this should scare the hell out of you. Was this election bought and paid for? Was this smoke and mirrors, sleight of hand? The more I listened to candidate Obama the less I heard. While we should have been paying attention to the issues we were fed gossip. Candidate Obama promised to reach across political differences while President-elect Obama appoints the most radical liberals to his cabinet. Instead of vetting his appointees we are discussing his possible dog. Just more smoke and mirrors to distract our attention from the real issues. Candidate Obama controlled the media with the skill of Kim Jung Il. But those of us who have been watching knew this all along.

Anyone who dares to question Obama or his qualifications has been crucified. Just look at Joe the Plumber. He asked a question and his background was investigated. Is this what we have to look forward to? Anyone that questioned the Obama Doctrine has been labeled racist, including Bill Clinton. How ironic is that? Will anyone who questions the Obama Doctrine be labeled a traitor? Will we be rounded up and put in concentration camps as political prisoners?

My sister calls more often now, as she says to make sure I haven't been assassinated. I told her what better cause to die for than freedom. Even if as Michelle Obama said in her tirade to African Press International, Barack Hussein Obama were to be proven to be adopted by his Indonesian father, the Rodney King/OJ factor will prevent the government from overturning the election. The government is so afraid of the race card and potential riots that they will ignore the Constitution. The Constitution says that you must be born in this country to be elected president. By being adopted by an Indonesian that would by law make him an Indonesian citizen and upon returning to the United States he would have become a

Naturalized citizen and thus ineligible for the presidency. Part of this is because at the time Obama would have been adopted, Indonesia did not allow dual citizenship. But as I said the government is too afraid of the race card. There are also rumors that Barack Obama was born in Kenya and that his Kenyan grandmother claims to have been at the hospital in Kenya where he was born. Reporters have been banned from contacting her. Like I say it is a rumor. The truth hidden in a fog of smoke and mirrors.

What next? Should we amend the Constitution to allow Arnold Schwarzenegger to run? There is a petition to do this. This is one of the problems with a president who has said he will appoint judges that will legislate for the Supreme Court. Not interpret the law but rewrite the law. President-elect Obama wants to appoint judges to the Supreme Court that will rewrite the Constitution. As I read the Constitution it says the Supreme Court has jurisdiction over disputes between individual states and Real Estate law only. Somewhere this law got lost in the legislation.

A few years ago a friend Diane Hooker-Roan, daughter of late blues great John Lee Hooker, emailed me saying Webster had changed the meaning of the N word. I told her not to forget the people who died because of that word.

The word Digger is a term that was used to denigrate the Native American in the late 19th and early 20th century but is now it means nothing more than the name of the local throw away paper. When we forget the true meaning of the word we also forget the hatred and bigotry that went along with it. Therefore change history. The more you hate the word the more you need to fight for the freedom of speech that is guaranteed in the Constitution. Some words that we have forgotten the meaning of are Marxist, Socialist, privacy, self-determination, independence, Democracy and even the true meaning of Freedom. The Liberals even want to change the meaning of the word marriage.

Why does one word incite such violence, why does one word make it a hate crime? Will the "D" (Democrat) word become the next "N" word? 85% of African American voters voted for Obama. Therefore 85% of African Americans can be seen as Socialists, Marxists or Communists. This is the dichotomy. I don't hate blacks but I hate Communists. Do you see the dilemma?

Obama's control can be illustrated by the suppression of the media combined with his condemnation of FOX. Obama has made statements that he doesn't believe the police force is sufficient to keep Americans safe, so President-elect Obama said he wants to draft a civilian paramilitary. Not a well armed militia but a paramilitary. Get a clue people, this sounds like at least two organizations that I know of one is the KGB. The other is the SS. The Democrats have purposed cutting defense spending by 25%. This is defense spending, not war funding. President-elect Obama wants to eliminate the Strategic Air Defense, increase the war in Afghanistan and increase the number of troupes in the military. The money he says we will save in Iraq will only go toward the war effort in Afghanistan. We have a voluntary military now, but with reduced funding, funding that will eliminate enlistment bonuses, the military will not be able to attract the people that enlist now. Then what? The only way he can increase troupes in the military is to institute the draft. We are not turning qualified people away. Obama says he will talk to our enemies and this shouldn't surprise us. His friendships prove he has no compunction towards dealing with whomever will further his political career. His speech as President-elect shows he is already running for his second term even before he is sworn into office. Personally, I want my president to be able to pass a basic DOD security clearance. With Obama's associates he couldn't.

President-elect Obama and the Democrats want to eliminate the secret ballot for Union elections. Their idea is that this will increase the support for unions or so they say, but I think it will result in voter intimidation similar to that which occurred during the Kennedy and Johnson administrations. First it will be the union ballots, then we will be forced to caucus to vote for president. Then President Obama will try to suspend elections like Putin did because it is a tumultuous time.

We need to revamp the voting system to eliminate caucus. This is the most discriminating voting processes, leads to voter intimidation, and disenfranchises the elderly, the disabled, and the shift worker. Just look at the whole process. We must have secret ballots in all elections including primaries and union elections.

Now President-elect Obama wants to rebuild our infrastructure with his New New

Deal, and I am all for that. Our infrastructure is crumbling. But the Democrats have put so many environmental restrictions in place that it is impossible to move forward on any construction project without twenty years of evaluation, red-legged frog assessment, beaver relocation etc. President-elect Obama is said to want Robert F Kennedy Jr. to head the EPA. If he does that things will only get worse. Robert F Kennedy Jr. backed by Nancy Pelosi and Harry Reid. Nancy Pelosi told George Stephanopoulos that the reason she would not allow an up or down vote on drilling was *"**because we have a planet to save.**"* Forced to allow the moratorium on offshore drilling a Democratic ran Congress under an Obama administration will reinstitute a ban on offshore drilling.

In California the Democratic ran Senate refuses to allow construction of desperately needed water storage facilities. They won't allow hydroelectric power plants even though President-elect Obama supports hydroelectric energy which is clean, renewable and safe because it might displace a deer population. They want to tie construction to your carbon footprint. To prevent development outside their area of control. They want to force feed solar energy at a cost of $4000 to $5000 per kilowatt, a product that takes more wattage to manufacture than it can produce, that starts to die in as little as eight years, long before it can recover the purchase cost. They want to force us into CNG so they can line their pockets. If you want to restrict your movements to 25 to 40 miles per day, then buy into CNG. Buy into electric cars. Living off the grid on solar you are forced to augment your panels with a fossil fuel generator and utilize lead acid batteries. These are all environmental contaminates. Where are these batteries and panels going to be recycled? Too often the batteries end up in creeks, transportation costs offsetting the recycling value. Living off the grid requires cutting trees and causes a tremendous amount of erosion. The government and environmentalists don't tell you about this because they are reaping financial benefits. But we have the protected spotted owl. The result the forests are consumed in massive wildfires. It makes no economic sense except to those lining their pockets. Like Deep Throat said *"Follow the money trail."*

Under President-elect Obama's redistribution of wealth we may as well give everybody their own home free. This

160

certainly would take the bad mortgages off the market, give everybody a place to live and kill our economy. When Barney Franks gets up and tells Congress that Freddie Mac and Fannie Mae are sound and we don't need to fix something that isn't broken while having a relationship which is an obvious conflict of interest. Clearly Barney Franks and friend Chris Dodd did not follow the Rules of the House.[6] The ethic rules that govern our government. The issues that caused the mortgage meltdown were created in the Carter and Clinton Administrations. But don't worry, the top 5% will pay to fix it as well as our economic stimulus package and our healthcare. Oh excuse me, our health insurance. Because under President-elect Obama's plan you are not guaranteed healthcare, you get health insurance. Special Interests at work here too. I have health insurance but it is very difficult finding a doctor that will accept it. Doctors come out of school with a tremendous amount of debt which they then pass on to the patient with exorbitant healthcare costs. The only way to reduce healthcare costs is to eliminate insurance, pay for the education and hire the doctors as federal employees. This is

---

[6] http://ethics.house.gov/

socialized medicine. President-elect Obama's plan is for socialized insurance not healthcare.

I believe in the total separation of church and state. Candidate Obama told George Stephanopoulos in an interview *"I'm glad you didn't hold my Muslim religion against me."* George Stephanopoulos corrected him by saying you mean your Christian religion and Obama responded *"Yah my Christian religion."* Now if he is a Christian why would he think people would hold his religion against him? I don't care what religion a person is. Just don't lie about it. I walked out of my church in 1967 when the minister started preaching hate. Yet Obama sat silent for twenty years, not hearing, not seeing, not speaking any evil apparently sleeping through Jeremiah's Wright's sermons. That is until it is politically expedient to disavow him. In Wright's latest interview he said there was no rift between the two of them. So what's the truth? We just don't know.

Americans are in dept $500,000,000,000 to China, and President-elect Obama wants to add a trillion dollars to our national dept. His economic plans will bankrupt the country. He wants to increase capital gains

162

taxes up to 50%. He wants to eliminate your 401K and force you to put your savings into Social Security which he will pay a 3% return.

This sounds like the Karl Marx Communist Doctrine to me. I listen to the economists, and people like Trump and Forbes. They predict dire straits under President Obama. Donald Trump says economic depression. I agree. Personally I think under an Obama administration Wall Street will drop below 2000 points, unemployment will exceed 10%, worldwide food shortages will occur and our national dept will exceed three trillion dollars. We are already seeing some of these things come to pass. This is why I voted for John McCain. Can anyone out there tell me why they voted for Obama?

January 6, 2009, New York Democrat, Congressman Jose Serrano introduced bill H. J. Res. 5, which was referred to the U.S. House Committee on the Judiciary for consideration. This measure would repeal the Constitution's 22nd Amendment prohibiting a president from being elected to more than two terms in office. According to the bill's language, it proposes "an amendment to the Constitution of the

United States to repeal the twenty-second article of amendment. To do so would remove the limitation on the number of terms an individual may serve as President." 7

Asked if he plans to introduce the legislation again in 2009, Rangel said, "Probably ... yes. I don't want to do anything this early to distract from the issue of the economic stimulus."8 Isn't this what Hugo Chavez wants to do? To rewrite and suspend the Constitution (of Venezuela). Isn't that what Putin is trying to do? Ultimate power . . .

Why is it that it takes the states to ratify a Constitutional Amendment but we don't get to vote on overturning it? We couldn't even ratify the Equal Rights Amendment. Here is one for you Amendment 12 says **"But in choosing the President, the votes shall be taken by states, the representation from each state having one vote:"** I take that to mean the Electoral College has one vote per state. Not some magic number but a finite number. One for one. They Congress, read

---

7

http://www.govtrack.us/congress/billtext.xpd?bill=hj 111-5
8 MSNBC news
http://www.msnbc.msn.com/id/15805957/

it that they can have as many representatives who only have one vote.

Not an Option

"The world is going to see an African leading the biggest most powerful democracy in the world. This is all that matters."
Donna Brazile.

When Americans believe they have given all they can give Obama Press Secretary Robert Gibbs says "American people are all going to have to give some." Obama says he is "hopeful that this nation will endure." Failure is not an option. What is the worst that can happen? The demise of Freedom is not an acceptable solution to economic failure. Communism and Socialism are not options. The economy is on a downhill slide much like an avalanche. Congress cannot stop the meltdown by building a funeral pyre underneath the snow and throwing trillions of dollars at it. The problem with the Obama solution is the economy will fail regardless of the bailout because it is a market correction and would have been seen that way were it not for Paulson's Congressional testimony. Inflation, gas prices and home market values have gotten out of control. By adding trillions in deficit spending it will only made the situation worse. The economic meltdown of 2008 will be forever known as the Obama Depression.

Gas prices came down slightly before the election. Oil prices are down to the low $30 dollar range. The lowest in over a year yet gas prices have started creeping up. Why. A Democratic Congress that has indicated they will reinstate a ban on offshore drilling. President-elect Obama has recently changed his mind on letting the Bush tax credits expire. This is to Wall Street a small ray of hope. A carrot dangled in front of the starving masses.

January 20th, 2009, President Obama is sworn in. The Dow drops 332.13 points, S&P drops 44.90, NASDAQ drops 88.47.

The beginning . . .

"A democracy will continue to exist up until the time that voters discover they can vote themselves generous gifts from the public treasury. From that moment on, the majority always vote for the candidates who promise the most benefits from the public treasury, with the result that every democracy will finally collapse due to loose fiscal policy, which is always followed by a dictatorship."

167

~ Alexander Tyler, history professor at the
University of Edinburgh, Scotland, 1787

Epilog:

The government's job is to work for the people not the other way around. Its time they did their job and we hold them accountable.

There is a difference between listening and hearing. Obama listens but he doesn't hear.

You might ask yourself, "What can I do?" Don't take anything I say for fact. Check it out for yourself and then make up your own mind. Take the time to get involved. Write Congress. Write your Governor and your local representatives. Inform yourself on the issues before you vote.

Everything in this book is true. Or not? Everything contained within these pages is based upon quotes that I personally watched and listen to on video tape and on news media and internet research. The conclusions are my own conclusions not Sean Hannity's or FOX New's. How can you trust the media?

We have come a long way but we will never obtain equal rights until we quit talking about the first black or the first woman or the first Hispanic or the first

whatever and start talking about human
rights and a person's qualifications.